T0329188

THE EAST AFRICAN TAX SYSTEM

Rup Khadka

MKUKI NA NYOTA
DAR – ES – SALAAM

PUBLISHED BY
Mkuki na Nyota Publishers Ltd
P. O. Box 4246
Dar es Salaam, Tanzania
www.mkukinanyota.com

© Rup Khadka, 2015

ISBN: 978-9987-75-329-1

Visit www.mkukinanyota.com to read more about and to purchase any of Mkuki na Nyota books. You will also find featured authors, interviews and news about other publisher/author events. Sign up for our e-newsletters for updates on new releases and other announcements.

Dedicated to
the late John King, Senior Economist,
International Monetary Fund

Contents

Foreword[1]

During December 2014, the East African Tax and Governance Network (EATGN) wrote an open letter to the Heads of State and Minister of Finance of the East African Community (EAC) on behalf of civil society organisations of member countries. The letter urged the authorities to increase their efforts to end illicit financial flows and harmful tax incentives in the EAC. Whilst recognising the efforts made thus far in reducing and phasing out harmful tax incentives, the EATGN asserted that more work needs to be done, especially with regard to the transparency with which incentives are granted.

The opening paragraph of this foreword is apt, as, apart from discerning the broad concerns of civil society in the EAC region, it is a pointer for the need to understand the current state of tax systems within the region. Whilst standalone EAC country information about taxation rules and regulations is available to the general public, as well as publications by professional accounting firms, a technical assistance provider's overview (that Rup Khadka brings) contributes to the knowledge and perspective of the EAC region's current taxation systems and practices.

The book provides an easy-to-read overview of the tax systems in the EAC region and, in the process, challenges the mind to discern

---

1   The views expressed in this Foreword are those of the contributor and do not represent those of the International Monetary Fund or its policies.

and enquire into: cross-system/country comparisons, the rationale for each of the countries adopting the policies and approaches that they have in place, and the what, why and when near-full tax policy and system harmonisation across the countries will take place – recognising that full harmonisation is not easy to achieve. As a running economic community integration theme, calls for harmonisation of tax policies and legislation across the EAC region are being made. For example, at an October 2014 East African Business Summit in Kigali, the benefits for trade and investment of uniform tax policies and systems were prominently highlighted by the region's private sector.

But other than government officials, tax professionals, interest groups and ardent followers of tax systems within the EAC region, does the majority of the EAC citizenry understand what tax systems obtain in the region? Are the legislators, at both national and regional levels, up-to-date with these systems? Are the region's research institutes and networks (the EATGN states on its website that it does most of its research in Kenya), academicians and students of taxation following closely the developments and cross-cutting tax policy and system changes in the region? What are the fundamentals underpinning the EAC tax systems?

This book outlines for the reader the nature of the EAC tax jurisdictions, the taxes levied at the national and local government levels and the broad characteristics of these taxes: value added tax, excise duties, customs duties, personal income tax, and business profits tax. As an example of the latter case, the concepts of chargeable/taxable income, itemised versus non-itemised deductions, the treatment of capital costs, loss carry over and the different provisions across the countries and that of residency are explained. These issues should, again, whet the reader's appetite to not only understand current practices, but also to enquire into the rationale of why the tax regimes are set out in their current form.

As a former tax administration senior manager (in the Uganda Revenue Authority) and currently in my role as part of a team at the International Monetary Fund that provides tax administration technical assistance to various countries, I find the fundamentals elucidated in the book as a necessary value-adding baseline to the EAC (or any) tax system. As I read through the various chapters, the common inquisitive thread is: what are the facts, how do each of these countries compare against each other, what good practices are being implemented, what can these countries learn from each other, and because of the common interest and goals espoused by the EAC protocol, how can tax system harmonisation be catalysed – using the following perspectives: policy, legal, organisational, people skills and competencies, processes and procedures, and leveraging technological developments? In other words, how can the foregoing elements (and their linkages/interdependencies) be harnessed to achieve the goal of adequately financing public goods and services across the EAC countries?

This book achieves the aim of broadly outlining the characteristics and workings of the EAC tax systems. It serves as a very good reference point for legislators, government officials, researchers and students of taxation. It is a pointer to (and raises) a number of research questions for which further cross-cutting EAC tax system analytical work is needed, and by its very nature, contributes to the debate of the required next steps to resolving the tax harmonisation issues in the region. Rup Khadka plans to tackle some of the analytical issues that he has already whetted our appetite for in sequels to this publication. I commend this book to you.

Justin Zake
Tax Administration Diagnostic Tool (TADAT) Secretariat
Fiscal Affairs Department
International Monetary Fund
Washington DC
United States of America

Acknowledgments

This book is largely based on internet research. I benefited from informative publications by the International Bureau of Fiscal Documentation, Amsterdam and its excellent taxation database and also from the good collection of books on taxation at the National Institute of Public Finance and Policy, New Delhi's library; I am beholden to both institutions.

Stan Beesley offered meticulous comments on the first, second, third, sixth and seventh chapters; Mukul G. Asher provided useful comments on the fourth chapter, Sijbren Cnossen on the fifth chapter, Horst Zimmermann on the seventh chapter, and Arthur Mann on the eighth chapter; I am extremely indebted to all of them. I am grateful to Munawer Sultan Khwaja for his valuable feedback, which benefited the book on the whole.

I am indebted to Justin Zake for reviewing the manuscript and writing a Foreword for the book, Rita Wadhwa for editing, and Mkuki Na Nyota Publishers for bringing it out as a publication.

I would also like to thank the editors of the *Bulletin for International Taxation* and the *International VAT Monitor* for publishing my articles on the East African Community tax administration and East African Community value added tax systems, respectively in their popular journals.

My special thanks are due to my wife Anita for making me free from household matters and taking on herself an immeasurable burden during the preparation of this study. This piece of work would never have been initiated and completed without her constant inspiration and cooperation. My son Utsab and daughter Upasana also deserve my gratitude for their constant inspiration to complete this volume.

Rup Khadka
Kathmandu, Nepal
December, 2014

List of Tables

Acronyms

ASEAN	Association of South East Asian Nations
ASYCUDA	Automated System for Customs Data
BPT	Business Profit Tax
BRA	Burundi Revenue Authority
EAC	East African Community
EACMA	East African Excise Management Act
EACCMA	East African Community Customs Management Act
EPZ	Export Processing Zone
EU	European Union
GDP	Gross Domestic Product
GST	Goods and Services Tax
KRA	Kenya Revenue Authority
LTO	Large Taxpayer Office
OECD	Organization for Economic Cooperation and Development
PE	Permanent Establishment
PIT	Personal Income Tax
RRA	Rwanda Revenue Authority
SARA	Semi-Autonomous Revenue Authority
PCA	Post Clearance Audit
PSI	Pre-Shipment Inspection
SAARC	South Asian Association for Regional Cooperation

TIN	Taxpayer Identification Number
TRA	Tanzania Revenue Authority
URA	Uganda Revenue Authority
UNCTAD	United Nations Conference on Trade and Development
UN	United Nations
VAT	Value Added Tax
WTO	World Trade Organization

Chapter 1

Introduction

1.1 Background

The East African Community (EAC), with headquarters in Arusha, Tanzania, is a regional intergovernmental organisation of five East African Nations vis., Burundi, Kenya, Rwanda, Tanzania and Uganda. While Kenya, Tanzania and Uganda have been founder members of the EAC since its inception in 2000, Burundi and Rwanda joined the group in 2007.

The EAC region covers an area of 1,817.7 thousands square kilometres or 0.36% of the world's total surface area. The EAC has a share of almost 1.93% of the world population (2011 figures) and less than a quarter of this population lives in urban areas (see Table 1.1).

Table 1.1: Geographic and Demographic Situation of EAC Countries

Country	Total Surface Area (000's Km2) 2011	Total Population (Million) 2011	Population Density (Per Sq. Km) 2011	Urban population as % of total population*	Life Expectancy at birth (years) 2011	Literacy rate % 2011
Burundi	27.8	8.7	312.2	11	50	60
Kenya	582.7	38.6	67.6	22	55	62
Rwanda	26.3	10.7	406.3	19	52	70
Tanzania	939.3	44.5	50.3	26	55	70
Uganda	241.6	32.9	164.7	13	50	73

Sources: East African Community Facts and Figures (2012), East African Community Secretariat, Arusha, Tanzania (September 2012), and CIA, The World Fact Book.

Table 1.2: Economic Situation of EAC Countries

Country	Income category	Composition of GDP		Per capita GDP in 2012	Population below poverty	Labour force absorbed by
		Agriculture	Non-agriculture			
Burundi	Low income	31.1	68.9	600	68%	94%
Kenya	Lower middle income	24.2	75.9	1,800	50%	75%
Rwanda	Lower middle income	33.3	66.7	1,400	45%	90%
Tanzania	Lower middle income	27.1	72.97	1,700	36%	80%
Uganda	Lower middle income	23.9	76.1	1,400	24%	82%

Source: CIA, The World Fact Book.

Of the EAC countries, Burundi is a low income country and the others fall under the category of lower middle income countries. In 2012, Gross Domestic Product (GDP) per capita ranged from USD 600 in Burundi to USD 1,800 in Kenya.

Agriculture accounts for about one quarter to one third of GDP in the EAC countries. On average, more than 80% of the total labour force is absorbed by this sector. In this region, a large part of the population lies below the poverty level.

Most of the countries in East Africa are rich in natural resources. For example, Kenya, Tanzania and Uganda have oil, while Burundi and Tanzania have gold, diamonds and gemstones.

1.2 Evolution

In respect of evolutionary development, the EAC is the fastest growing regional intergovernmental organisation. Major developments are listed below:

Table 1.3: Evolution of the EAC

Date	
1961	Establishment of the East African Common Services Organisation by Kenya, Tanganyika (Tanzania) and Uganda.
1967	Creation of the EAC in place of the East African Common Services Organisation.
1977	The EAC dissolved.
1993	Kenya, Tanzania and Uganda signed the Treaty for East African Co-operation.
1999	Treaty for the Establishment of the EAC signed by Kenya, Tanzania and Uganda.
2000	Treaty for the Establishment of the EAC came into force after its ratification by Kenya, Tanzania and Uganda, i.e. EAC came into existence.
2004	Protocol for Establishment of the EAC Customs Union signed.
2005	Customs Union established.
2007	Burundi and Rwanda joined the EAC.
2010	Common Market protocol entered into force.
2011	Negotiations began for the creation of a Monetary Union.
2013	Protocol for the Establishment of the EAC Monetary Union signed.

Source: EAC. History of the EAC, see http://www.eac.int/index.

1.3 Economic integration

EAC partner states are committed to integrate their economies. There are four pillars of integration, which are as follows:

1.3.1 Customs Union

Encyclopaedia Britannica defines customs union as "a trade agreement by which group of countries charge a common set of tariffs to the rest of the world while granting free trade among them." It is a kind of bloc where trade takes place freely without internal tariffs between the members of the bloc. Member states, however, levy common external tariffs on goods entering the union.

In the EAC region, a Protocol for the Establishment of the Customs Union was signed by the Heads of States of Kenya, Tanzania and Uganda on 2 March 2004 and the Customs Union was established in 2005. Rwanda and Burundi joined the Customs Union in 2008 and began its implementation in July 2009. The Union became fully-fledged in January 2010. Under this arrangement, member states agreed to levy a 3-band common external tariff with a minimum rate of 0% on raw materials, a middle rate of 10% on semi-processed goods and a maximum rate of 25% on finished goods. They also agreed not to levy any internal tariffs and remove all non-tariff barriers on inter-Union trade. The establishment of the Customs Union was the first stage of the regional integration process in the EAC region.

1.3.2 Common Market

EAC defines common market as "a merger/union of two or more territories to form one common territory in which there is free movement of goods, labour, services and capital, and the right of establishment and residence."[1] The free movement of goods, services, labour and capital is expected to boost trade and investment in the community. The Protocol on the establishment of the EAC Common Market was signed by the Heads of State on 20 November 2009 and came into force on 1 July 2010. Establishment of the EAC Common Market is the second stage of the regional integration process. There are other common markets in different parts of the world. The European Common market is a classic example.

---

1   EAC. http://www.eac.int/commonmarket/what-it-is.html.

1.3.3. Monetary Union

Under the monetary union, two or more countries share the same currency. For example, under the European Monetary Union, the Euro is used as the national currency of the Eurozone and surrounding countries. South East Asian countries are planning to create a monetary union by 2015 when this region will adopt an Asian Monetary Union as a single currency of the member countries of the Association of South East Asian Nations (ASEANs). EAC countries are working on the draft of an EAC Monetary Union Protocol. The EAC Monetary Union is expected to be established in 2024[2] when this region adopts the East African Shilling as a common currency of the member countries. This will be an important step in the integration process.

1.3.4 Political Federation

The EAC's ultimate goal is to become a political federation of East African Nations. The matter is under discussion. This will be the final step in the integration process. "The Treaty for the Establishment of the EAC provides for fundamental principles that shall govern the achievement of the objectives of the community which include mutual trust, political will and sovereign equality, peaceful coexistence and good neighbourliness, peaceful settlement of disputes."[3]

1.4 Fiscal scenario

The fiscal scenario of the EAC countries is presented in Tables 1.4 and 1.5. Recurrent expenditure is higher than development expenditure in each country. Government revenue constitutes both domestic revenue and grants. Domestic revenue comes from tax and non-tax sources. These countries also receive grants from international development partners. All the EAC countries face budget deficit which is met through domestic as well as external sources.

---

2   EAC. http://www.eac.int/index.php?option=com_content&view=article&id=1601:-tanzania-becomes-first-partner-state-to-ratify-eac-monetary-union-protocol&catid=146:press-releases&Itemid=194.

3   EAC. http://www.eac.int/index.php.

Table 1.4: Government Budgetary Operations (in Million USD)

Description	2011/12				
	Burundi	Kenya	Rwanda	Tanzania	Uganda
Government Total Expenditure	498	12,041	1,783	8,564	3,624
Government Recurrent Expenditure	328	8,611	998	5,445	2,755
Government Development Expenditure	170	3,430	785	3,119	869
Government Revenue	665	9,860	1,705	6,011	3,034
Domestic Sources	538	9,680	962	4,290	2,593
Tax	350	7,923	905	3,944	2,398
Non-Tax	188	1,757	57	346	195
Grants	127	180	743	1,721	441
Budget Deficit (including Grants)	167	(2,181)	(78)	(2,553)	(590)
Budget Deficit (Excluding Grants)	40	(2,361)	(821)	(4,274)	(1,031)

Source: EAC Website

As indicated in Table 1.5, the ratio of total expenditure to GDP ranged from 18.1% in Uganda to 35.4% in Kenya in 2012. In the same year, the Tax/GDP ratio ranged from 12.3% in Uganda to 19.7% in Kenya. There are big variations in the ratio of deficit to GDP between these countries. For example, deficit/GDP ratio was lowest at 1.2% in Rwanda and highest in Tanzania (5.6%).

Table 1.5: Selected Macro Economic Indicators to GDP, percent

Description	2012				
	Burundi	Kenya	Rwanda	Tanzania	Uganda
Total expenditure to GDP	26.6	35.4	26.8	25.8	18.1
Recurrent expenditure to GDP	19.1	24.0	15.0	18.0	10.9
Development expenditure to GDP	7.4	9.6	11.8	7.9	7.2

Tax revenue to GDP	15.2	19.7	13.6	15.6	12.3
Revenue excluding. grants to GDP	16.4	26.7	14.5	17.0	13.3
External grants to GDP	7.1	1.5	11.2	3.2	2.3
Budget deficit/ surplus to GDP	(3.1)	(5.3)	(1.2)	(5.6)	(3.0)
Budget deficit/ surplus excluding grants to GDP	(10.2)	(6.9)	(12.4)	(8.9)	(5.3)

Source: EAC (2013). East African Community Facts and Figures.

1.5 Relative importance of taxes

The relative importance of various taxes in the selected EAC countries is given in Tables 1.6, 1.7, and 1.8. As indicated in these tables, income taxes (personal income tax – PIT and business profit tax – BPT combined) are the largest sources of tax revenue followed by value added tax (VAT). Income taxes provided 46.42% of total tax revenue in Kenya and 31.34% of total tax revenue in Tanzania in 2010/11, while their share in the total tax revenue was 35.32% in Uganda in 2011/12. VAT's share in the total tax revenue was 28.91% in Tanzania, 30.85% in Kenya and 32.11% in Uganda. Excise duties provided almost a quarter of total tax revenue in Uganda, while their share in total tax revenue was 14.46% in Kenya and 19.86% in Tanzania. Surprisingly, in all these countries customs duties provided about 8% of total tax revenue.

Table 1.6: Relative Importance of Taxes in Kenya 2010/11

Taxes	Revenue collection (Billions of KES)	Tax revenue as percent of		
		Total Tax Revenue	Total Revenue	GDP
VAT	171.9	30.85	25.75	6.2
Excise duties	80.6	14.46	12.07	2.9
Income taxes	258.7	46.42	38.76	9.3
Customs duties	46.1	8.27	6.91	1.7
Total	557.2	100.0	83.49	20.1

Source: IMF (2012). *IMF Country Report.* 12/300, November.

Tax revenue constituted 92.27% of total revenue in Tanzania in 2010/11. The corresponding figure was 90.15% in Uganda in 2011/12 and 83.49% in Kenya in 2010/11.

Table 1.7: Relative Importance of Taxes in Tanzania 2010/11

Taxes	Revenue collection (Billions of TZS)	Tax revenue as percent of		
		Total Tax Revenue	Total Revenue	GDP
VAT	1,531	28.91	26.68	4.4
Excise duties	1,052	19.86	18.33	3.0
Income taxes	1,660	31.34	28.92	4.8
Customs duties	449	8.48	7.82	1.3
Others	604	11.40	10.52	1.7
Total	5,296	100.00	92.27	15.2

Source: IMF (2013). IMF Country Report. 13/12, January.

In the selected EAC countries, tax/GDP ratio ranged from 12% in Uganda in 2011/12 to 20% in Kenya in the same fiscal year. Income tax/GDP ratio in Kenya was little over 9% while in Tanzania and Uganda it was over 4%. VAT/GDP ratio is about 4% in Tanzania and Uganda and 6% in Kenya.

Table 1.8: Relative Importance of Taxes in Uganda 2011/12

Taxes	Revenue collection (Billions of UGX)	Tax revenue as percent of		
		Total Tax Revenue	Total Revenue	GDP
VAT	1,921	32.11	28.95	3.9
Excise duties	1,446	24.17	21.79	2.9
Income taxes	2,112	35.32	31.83	4.2
Customs duties	503	8.41	7.58	1.0
Total	5,983	100.00	90.15	12.0

Source: IMF (2013). IMF Country Report. 13/25, January.

1.6 Tax regime

All the EAC member states levy limited broad based taxes, vis. VAT, excise duties, customs duties, PIT and BPT at the national level. There appear to be no significant nuisance taxes, which generate high costs without corresponding revenue gains.

Table 1.9: National Tax System of the EAC Countries

Burundi	Kenya	Rwanda	Tanzania	Uganda
VAT	VAT	VAT	VAT	VAT
ED	ED	ED	ED	ED
CD	CD	CD	CD	CD
PIT	PIT	PIT	PIT	PIT
BPT	BPT	BPT	BPT	BPT

VAT = Value Added Tax, ST = Sales Tax, ED = Excise Duties, CD = Customs Duties, PIT = Personal Income Tax, and BPT = Business Profit Tax.

1.6.1 Value added tax

All EAC countries have adopted a standard destination-based consumption type tax credit method VAT with a simple rate structure. Rwanda, Tanzania and Uganda have adopted a single positive rate of 18%. Burundi also had levied VAT at a uniform rate of 18% until 2012, but adopted a lower rate of 10% in 2013 for agricultural products, livestock and food imports, whilst maintaining the standard rate at 18%. Kenya has adopted a standard rate of 16% and a lower rate of 12% on the supply and import of electricity and fuels. EAC countries zero-rate exports as well as some other specified commodities to relieve them from the VAT burden. As mentioned later in Section 4.3.2, they have also exempted many goods and services from VAT.

EAC countries collect VAT at all stages in the process of production and distribution. This means that importers, manufacturers, wholesalers and retailers, above the registration threshold, are required to register for the purpose of VAT. They must collect tax on their sales and deduct the tax paid on their purchases from the tax collected on sales and remit the difference to the treasury as VAT. A bird's eye view of EAC VATs is given in table 1.10.

Table 1.10: A Bird's Eye View of EAC VATs

Description	Burundi	Kenya	Rwanda	Tanzania	Uganda
Tax Law	Value Added Tax Act 2009	Value Added Tax Act 1989	Value Added Tax Code 2001	Value Added Tax Act 1997	Value Added Tax Act 1996
Principle	Destination	Destination	Destination	Destination	Destination
Type	Consumption	Consumption	Consumption	Consumption	Consumption
Method of computation	Tax credit	Tax credit	Tax credit	Tax credit	Tax credit
Exemptions	Many	Many	Many	Many	Many
Rate %	18, 10	16, 14	18	18	18
VAT Productivity*	0.49	0.36	0.23	0.29	0.20
Zero rating	Exports and specified items	Exports and specified items	Exports and specified items	Exports and specified items	Exports and specified items
Annual Threshold	BIF 100 million (USD64,808)	KES 5 million (USD56,179)	RWF 20 million (USD29,368)	TZS 40 million (USD23,474)	UGX 50 million (USD18,234)
Threshold: Retrospective basis					
Threshold: Prospective basis	NA		NA		
Voluntary registration					
Standard Tax Period	Calendar month	Calendar month	Calendar month	Calendar month	Calendar month
Date of filing	15th of the following month	20th day of the following month	15th day of the following month	30th day of the following month	15th day of the following month
Date of payment	15th of the following month	20th day of the following month	15th day of the following month	30th day of the following month	15th day of the following month

Source: USAID. http://egateg.usaid.gov/collecting-taxes.

1.6.3 Customs duties

EAC countries do not levy internal tariffs on the import of goods produced within EAC member states. They, however, do levy a three band common external tariff on imports from countries outside the EAC region. The level of tariff depends upon the finished stage of a product. For example, raw materials are subject to zero tariffs, semi-processed goods are subject to a lower rate and finished goods are subject to higher tariff. EAC members have adopted the Harmonised Commodity Description and Coding System (Harmonised System), which is required to be adopted by the member countries under the Protocol on the Establishment of the East African Customs Union. They follow the Agreement on Customs Valuation (ACV) system for the determination of customs duties.[4]

1.6.4 Personal income tax

EAC countries levy PIT on taxable income that includes all income received for the provision of labour or capital or both, of whatever form or nature. Income sources are broadly divided into three categories as employment, business and investment/property income. EAC countries largely levy tax on the worldwide income of a resident taxpayer, but only on the income from domestic sources in the case of a non-resident taxpayer. They have, in general, adopted a global system, where income received by a taxpayer is considered on a global basis and subject to progressive tax rates. They, however, levy separate tax on some sources of income. They also levy presumptive tax and withholding taxes.

PIT is levied on net income, which is obtained by deducting from the gross income business expenses and personal expenses. Besides, an initial amount of income is exempt from tax by means of a basic allowance/zero-rate bracket. PIT is levied with progressive rates on higher income in all EAC countries.

---

4   ACV focuses on the transaction value of imported goods, which is the price actually paid or payable. For details see Section 6.4.

Table 1.12: An Overview of PIT in the EAC Countries

Descriptions	Burundi	Kenya	Rwanda	Tanzania	Uganda
Tax law	General Tax Code	Income Tax Act 1974	Laws on Direct Taxes on Income 2005	Income Tax Act 2004	Income Tax Act 1997
Tax system (Global/ scheduler/ mixed system)	Mixed	Mixed	Mixed	Mixed	Mixed
Source vs. worldwide principle	Origin	Worldwide	Worldwide	Worldwide	Worldwide
Classification of income	Wage/salaries, capital gains, profits, agricultural income etc.	Income from business, employment, use of property, dividends, pension, royalties, interest, rent etc.	Employment, business and investment/ property income	Employment, business and investment/ property income	Employment, business and investment/ property income
Basic allowance/tax credit	BIF 1,800,000	KES 13,944 (tax credit)	RWF 360,000	TZS 2,040,000	UGX 2,820,000
Tax unit	Joint taxation	Individual taxation	Individual taxation	Individual taxation	Individual taxation
Tax rate	20% and 30%	10%, 15%, 20%, 25% and 30%	20% and 30%	13%, 20%,25% and 30%	10%, 20%, 30% and 40%
Presumptive system					

1.6.5 Business profit tax

BPT is levied on net income or profit of legal entities, which is calculated by deducting allowable business expenses from the gross income. All EAC countries, except Burundi, have adopted a general deduction system where they allow taxpayers to deduct all the business expenses incurred directly in earning the business income in the income year. Burundi, however, has adopted an itemised system of deduction, where the deductible items are specifically mentioned in the tax law and no deduction is allowed for any other item.

Costs of capital nature are not deductible since assets are used to generate income for more than one year. Instead, depreciation on capital assets may be deducted during the useful life of the assets. While EAC countries largely have adopted a pooled system of depreciation, Burundi has adopted an itemised system of depreciation where depreciable items are listed separately and depreciation rates are specified for each item in the tax law. All the EAC countries allow taxpayers to carry over losses and offset them against profits in future years, commonly five years.

Resident companies are required to pay tax on both domestic as well as foreign source incomes, while for non-resident companies only income from domestic sources is taken into account in all EAC countries. EAC countries generally levy BPT at a flat rate.

Table 1.13: An Overview of BPT in the EAC Countries

Descriptions	Burundi	Kenya	Rwanda	Tanzania	Uganda
Tax law	General tax code	Income tax act 1974	Laws on Direct Taxes on Income 2005	Income Tax Act 2004	Income Tax Act 1997
Expenses deduction system	Itemised	General	General	General	General
Depreciation system	Itemised System	Itemised system	Itemised system for buildings and pooled system for other assets	Pooled system	Itemised system for buildings and pooled system for other assets
Depreciation method	Straight-line as well as declining method	Choice of straight or declining method	Straight- line method	Straight-line method for buildings and intangibles, and diminishing balance method for others	Straight-line method for buildings and diminishing balance method for others
Loss carry back/forward	Carry forward 5 years	Carry forward 4 years	Carry forward 5 years	Carry forward indefinitely	Carry forward indefinitely
Rates	30%	30% residents, 37.5% non-residents	30%	25% (Newly listed companies) 30% Others	30%

1.7. Intergovernmental fiscal relations

EAC countries have adopted a unitary system of government where there are two tiers of government, national and local. Local governments again have different layers as follows:

Table 1.14: Local Government Systems in the EAC Countries

Country	Forms of Local Government	Local Taxes
Burundi	Provinces and communes	Property tax, vehicle tax
Kenya	Rural areas: Counties Urban areas: Towns, Municipalities and Cities	Property tax, Entertainment tax, User charges, Any other authorised tax by an Act of Parliament
Rwanda	Villages, Cells, Sectors and Districts	Property tax, Rental income tax, Trading licenses
Tanzania	Rural areas: Vitongoji/Hamlets, Villages and Districts Urban areas: Municipalities, Towns and Cities	Development levy, Head tax, Property tax, Service levy, Business license fee, Other fees and user charges
Uganda	Rural area: Villages, Parishes, Sub-counties, Counties, and Districts Urban areas: Wards, Towns, Municipalities, and Cities	Rents rates, royalties, Stamp duties, business licenses, and local hotel tax, Registration fees, Any other fees and taxes that Parliament may prescribe

There are similarities as well as differences in the taxes levied at the local level in the EAC countries. Local governments levy property taxes which are in line with the principles of local taxation and international good practices. In Rwanda and Uganda local governments also levy rent taxes. Local governments are also authorised to levy user charges and some fees. There are also some country specific taxes levied by the local governments in the EAC region.

Various levels of government have the authority to generate their own sources of revenue and decide how to use their revenue to provide public services. As EAC countries are implementing decentralisation programs, they have been transferring more and more expenditure responsibilities to the sub-national governments. As the local governments know the requirements of their constituents better than the national governments, they can tailor programs to match the demand of their constituency. This is expected to enhance efficiency.

However, tax assignments in these countries seem inappropriate since, as described in Chapter 7, major revenue sources are limited to the national level, but they have not been developed as shared taxes.

1.8 Tax administration

EAC members have created Semi-Autonomous Revenue Authorities (SARAs). EAC tax administrations have been organised as unified tax administrations with a mixed organisational structure, where functional focus is combined with the taxpayer segment focus. As mentioned in Chapter 8, tax bodies have been implementing medium-term corporate plans that define their visions, missions, values, objectives, activities and performance indicators.

1.9 Summary

The EAC is the regional intergovernmental organisation of five East African Countries, vis. Burundi, Kenya, Rwanda, Tanzania, and Uganda. Its surface area is 1.82 million square km, total population is 135.4 million and GDP per capita is USD 732. EAC member states are committed to integrate their economies by means of participating in a customs union, common market, and monetary union, and finally become a political federation of the East African Nations.

EAC countries have adopted a unitary system of government where there are two tiers of government: national and local. Both the national and local governments are authorised to levy various taxes. All the EAC countries levy VAT, excise duties, customs duties, PIT and BPT at the national level, while local governments are authorised to levy property based taxes, rental taxes, user charges and fees.

EAC member states have established semi-autonomous revenue authorities to implement their tax systems. They are organised as unified tax administrations with a mixed organisational structure, where functional focus is combined with the taxpayer segment focus. EAC tax administrations have been implementing medium-term corporate plans that define their visions, missions, values, objectives, activities and performance indicators.

EAC member states have been trying to harmonise their tax systems in order to make the tax policy/system similar within the EAC region. Their national tax systems are pretty much rationalised as these countries levy limited broad based taxes and there are no nuisance taxes, which is the main thrust of the modern tax reform. While customs duties are fully harmonised, VATs are also largely synchronised. There are, however, striking differences in the structure and operation of excise duties and income taxes of the EAC member states and there is a long way to go to fully harmonise the tax systems of these countries.

Chapter 2

Personal Income Tax

2.1. Introduction

All EAC partner states levy tax on the income of individuals. This tax is levied under the General Tax Code[1] in Burundi, Income Tax Act 1974 in Kenya, and Laws on Direct Taxes on Income 2005 in Rwanda. The tax is imposed under the Income Tax Act 2004 in Tanzania, which applies to both Tanzania Mainland as well as Tanzania Zanzibar. Law imposing income tax in Uganda is the Income Tax Act 1997.

Income tax, also known as individual income tax elsewhere, is called business tax in Burundi (though it is levied on employment, business and investment income of individuals), personal income tax in Rwanda, and is simply known as income tax in Kenya, Tanzania and Uganda. In this chapter, the tax will be called personal income tax, abbreviated as PIT.

PIT, in general, is levied on the income of individuals (natural persons and sole proprietorship businesses) for each income year, where income year is the calendar year in Burundi, Kenya, Rwanda and Tanzania, and July-June in Uganda. It is, however, possible to change the income year

---

1   As contained in the Law of 21 September 1963, as amended to date.

into any 12-month period with the approval of designated authorities such as the Finance Minister in Rwanda, and Commissioner in Tanzania and Uganda.

2.2. Coverage and classification of income

Payment made for the provisions of labour or capital, or combination of both, in whatever form, cash or kind, are taxable in the EAC region. It is to be noted that sometimes payments for the provision of labour are made in kind, not in cash. For example, an employer may provide vehicles, food, clothes, quarters and other benefits in kind to his employees instead of cash. While it is difficult to determine income for the payment made in kind, there is a practice, as discussed later on, to levy tax on fringe benefits. Ideally all incomes received in money or money's worth for the provision of labour or capital or both should be taxable, unless they are specifically exempt by law.For practical purposes, it is common in the EAC countries to define the scope of income for the purpose of income tax. These countries have tried to create a workable tax base, not an ideal tax base, where the taxable income includes all income received for the provision of labour or capital or both, of whatever form or nature. Furthermore, income tax laws of EAC countries define income as the income generated from specified sources, which are broadly divided into three categories as employment, business and investment/property income in Rwanda, Tanzania and Uganda.[2]

Of the above three categories of income, such incomes as wages, salary, payment in lieu of leave, bonus, gratuity or other allowances received in respect of employment or services rendered, retirement contributions and retirement payments, payment for redundancy or loss, or termination of employment, other payment made in respect of employment including benefits in kind, are included under employment income.

On the other hand, incomes like incomings for trading stock, gains from the realisation of business assets or liabilities of the business, service fees, amounts derived as consideration for accepting a restriction on the capacity to conduct business, gifts and other *ex gratia* payments are included under business income. As discussed later in Section 2.14,

---

2   Countries like Burundi and Kenya list taxable income in more individual categories of income. For example, income sources are listed as wages/salaries, capital gains, profits, agricultural income etc. in Burundi, while income from business, employment, use of property, dividends, pension, royalties, interest, rents etc. are included in Kenya.

long-term capital gains are included in the business income in some countries, while they are treated differently in other countries.

Other incomes such as dividend, interest, natural resource payment, rent or royalty, net gains from the realisation of investment assets, and amounts derived as consideration for accepting a restriction on the capacity to conduct the investment are part of investment/property income.

However, not all sources of income are subject to tax in the EAC countries, where common exemptions include exemptions of income of diplomats/foreign governments/United Nations (UN) officials, exemptions granted under international agreements, and exemptions provided under the contract signed by the government. Similarly, income of governments at different levels, as well as government of foreign countries, and income of religious or charitable organisations and trust bodies are exempt. Scholarships, fellowships, grants, gifts, and awards are also commonly exempt.

There are some specific exemptions provided for various purposes under the income tax law of different EAC countries, where governments are empowered to exempt any income from tax. For example, in Burundi, different sources of income, including commuting costs up to 15% of salary, housing allowances up to 60% of basic wage, annuities and payments granted under legislation governing old-age pensions, disability pensions, widows, orphans' and war pensions, pensions paid to victims of industrial accidents and to congenitally handicapped persons, and alimony and different types of rental incomes are exempt. In Rwanda, retirement contributions made by the employer on behalf of the employee to the state social security fund, pension payments made under the state social security system, retirement contributions made by the employer on behalf of the employee and contributions made by the employee to a qualified pension fund are exempt. Some of the exemptions provided in Tanzania include:

- pensions or gratuities granted in respect of wounds or disabilities caused in war and suffered by the recipients of such pensions or gratuities,

- a scholarship or education grant payable in respect of tuition or fees for full-time instruction at an educational institution,

- amounts derived by way of alimony, maintenance or child support under a judicial order or written agreement,

- amounts derived by way of gift, bequest or inheritance,

- amounts derived in respect of an asset that is not a business asset, depreciable asset, investment asset or trading stock,

- amounts derived by way of foreign living allowance by any officer of the Government that are paid from public funds and in respect of performance of the office overseas,
- amounts earned by non-residents on deposits in Banks registered by the Bank of Tanzania, and
- gratuity granted to a Member of Parliament at the end of each term.

Omission of various sources of income from the income tax net leads to an erosion of the tax base. Besides, exemption of some sources of income from the income tax net has several other consequences. For example, exclusion of some sources of income from income tax brings inequity since these sources are favoured against others. It also brings economic inefficiency since resources are likely to be diverted from taxed to untaxed sectors in response to tax. Omissions also provide loopholes for tax evasion and complicate tax administration. There is, therefore, a need to keep the exemptions at minimum.

2.3. Worldwide vs. source principle

Income tax can be levied on the basis of worldwide or source principle. Under the worldwide principle, tax is levied on the total income of a taxpayer, irrespective of its source. This means if a taxpayer has income in the country where he is a resident and also in other countries, he is required to pay tax on the total income obtained in different countries in his country of residence. On the other hand, under the source principle, a taxpayer is required to pay tax on the income generated in a country where he is a resident, not on income received from abroad. The common practice around the world is to levy tax on the basis of the worldwide principle in case of a resident taxpayer and source principle[3] in the case of a non-resident.

EAC countries also largely levy tax on the worldwide income of a resident taxpayer, but only on the domestic source income in the case of a non-resident taxpayer. While these countries do not define residents

---

3   It is to be noted that generally developing countries focus on the source principle. These countries import capital from the developed countries. They want to tax income earned within their territory even by the foreign investors to generate some revenue. They do not expect much revenue from the foreign source income of their residents as not only residents of these countries do not get much income from foreign sources, their tax rates in general are also lower than that of developed countries, which means developing countries are unlikely to get any revenue from foreign source income when they provide credit for taxes paid by their residents in other countries. Besides, the tax administrations of these countries are not equipped to obtain information about foreign source income of their residents and impose tax on it.

on the basis of nationality, they, among others, apply a physical presence test to define residents, where an individual is considered a resident if he is physically present in the country for at least a specified number of days in an income year. Details are presented in Table 2.1.

Table 2.1: Resident tests under the income tax laws of EAC Member States

Country	Description
An individual is a resident in Burundi for an income year if	s/he has established his effective and continuous place of residence in Burundi, regardless of his nationality;
	her/his home, family, place of business, work and main activities are in Burundi; or
	s/he has established his financial centre (place from which the individual administers his property) in Burundi.
An individual is a resident in Kenya for an income year if	s/he has a permanent home in Kenya and was present in Kenya for any period in a particular year of income under consideration; or
	s/he has no permanent home in Kenya but
	was present in Kenya for a period or periods amounting in the aggregate to 183 days or more in that year of income; or
	was present in Kenya in that year of income and in each of the two preceding years of income for periods averaging more than 122 days in each year of income;
An individual is a resident in Rwanda for an income year if	s/he has a permanent residence in Rwanda;
	s/he has a habitual abode in Rwanda;
	s/he is a Rwandan representing Rwanda abroad; or
	s/he stays in Rwanda for more than 183 days in any 12-month period, either continuously or intermittently, is resident in Rwanda for the tax period in which the 12 month period ends.
An individual is a resident in Tanzania for an income year if	s/he has a permanent home in Tanzania and is present in Tanzania during any part of the income year;
	s/he is present in Tanzania during the income year for a period or periods amounting in aggregate to 183 days or more;
	s/he is present in Tanzania during the income year and in each of the two preceding income years for periods averaging more than 122 days in each such income year; or
	s/he is an employee or an official of the government of the United Republic posted abroad during the income year.

Country	Description
An individual is a resident in Uganda for an income year if	s/he has permanent home in Uganda.
	s/he is present in Uganda
	for a period of, or periods amounting in total 183 days or more in any 12 month period; or
	during the income year and in each of the two preceding income years for periods averaging more than 122 days in each such income year.
	s/he is an employee or official of the government of Uganda posted abroad during the income years.

Sources: Income Tax Acts of the countries.

Taxpayers other than residents are non-residents.

In most EAC countries, resident taxpayers are required to pay tax on both domestic and foreign source income. Such a system is expected to create and/or protect the tax base by providing information about foreign income of the residents and encouraging domestic investors to invest in that country rather than in other countries, particularly some tax haven countries, thereby preventing flight of capital. Non-resident individuals are taxed only on their income from domestic sources.

Burundi, however, levied income tax on the basis of the source/ territoriality principle until 2012, when tax was levied only on income generated through the economic activities carried out within Burundi, both by residents and non-residents. Income received from sources outside Burundi was not taxable. Adoption of source principle by Burundi was understandable as the income tax system and tax administration were not matured and not much revenue was expected from sources outside Burundi. But since 2013, Burundi also switched to the worldwide taxation.

2.4. Global vs. scheduler system

EAC countries have, in general, adopted a global system, where income received by a taxpayer is considered on a global basis, not on source by source basis, for tax purposes. In other words, incomes received by a taxpayer from various sources are added together and after deducting allowable expenses, taxed jointly with a single progressive rate structure regardless of their sources. For example, in Uganda, all kinds of income are added together and the allowable deductions are subtracted from the gross income and tax is levied with a single progressive rate structure on the remaining income, which is known as chargeable income. Practice is similar in other EAC member countries.

Such a global system is desirable from an economic and equity point of view. Since income from all sources is taxed in the same manner, there is no need to divert resources from one sector to another in response to tax, and taxpayers are not encouraged to waste resources in tax planning. As the income from all sources is treated alike, the tax implication of any addition to the net income is the same irrespective of its source, which makes the tax system equitable.

In practice, it is not easy to implement a purely global system that treats all incomes in an equal manner, regardless of their sources. That is why some EAC countries levy a scheduler tax on specific sources of income, where income and expenditure are calculated by type of sources of income and are subject to separate tax rates. For example, Uganda levies a separate tax on rental income. For the purpose of the determination of the rental tax liability, 20% of the rental income is allowed as expenditures and losses incurred by the taxpayer in the production of rental income. The rate of tax is 20% of the chargeable income in excess of UGX 2,820,000.

Similarly, while investment income such as interest, dividends and royalties are subject to a separate flat tax of 15% in Rwanda, rental income is subject to a separate rental income tax at the sub-national level with a progressive rate structure ranging from 0% to 30% (i.e., 0%, 10%, 15%, 20%, 25% and 30%). Burundi also levies a separate tax on rental income with a separate exemption,[4] and deduction[5] system, and progressive rate structure.[6]

As discussed later, EAC countries also make extensive use of presumptive taxation and withholding taxes; several withholding taxes are final. For example, Uganda levies final withholding tax on payment of interest on treasury bills or other government securities issued by the Bank of Uganda to any person or a financial institution to a resident individual, and withholding tax on a payment of dividends to a resident individual. Tanzania has a large list of sources of income that are subject to final withholding tax.[7]

---

4   Exemptions include: rental income of state and local authorities, newly constructed buildings, one dwelling of an orphan or handicapped person, high rise building, or exempt under an international treaty.

5   A flat deduction of 40% of gross income, interest paid on the purchase of property generating rental income, improvement costs, and water and cleaning charges.

6   A total of 8 progressive rates, ranging from 20% to 60%.

7   See Appendix 2(a).

Thus EAC countries have been making use of a scheduler system to some extent, which provides some scope for differential tax treatment of various sources of income, depending upon the socio-economic conditions of the nation and, in some cases, is also used to check evasion by levying tax at source in the form of withholding or a separate tax in some flat manner.

The scheduler system, however, suffers from a number of limitations. To start with, since different sources of income are treated differently, the scheduler system gives rise to tax planning. Taxpayers may try to classify sources of income and expenses in such a way that it is most advantageous to them. It is difficult to have a proper idea of the structure and operation of income tax and its possible impact. It gives rise to the problem of definition and classification of income and expenses. As there are various deduction systems, expenses allowed under one type may be disallowed under the other. It further complicates tax administration since under this system taxpayers have to compute tax for each schedule separately and the tax administration has to check it. Furthermore, the scheduler income tax system is regressive in nature as the higher income groups have to pay less tax when the tax is assessed separately on various sources, instead of total income from all sources as their income is subject to lower marginal rates.

In reality, tax systems of various countries around the world are neither purely global nor scheduler. Rather, they are mixed. Some sources are subject to final withholding taxes, some sources are subject to presumptive tax, while still some others are subject to different taxes with different rate structure. Some sources are exempt, while some others are subject to reduced rates. In practice, even all the sources brought under the global tax system may not be treated in a similar manner due to ineffective tax administration, and tax avoidance and evasion. This is also true in the EAC region where PITs consist of the features of both global and scheduler tax[8] and can best be seen as a quasi-global system.

2.5. Deductions

EAC countries allow certain deductions under the PIT systems in respect of business expenses and personal expenses as follows:

---

8   The third possibility is the composite system where a global tax is levied on total income from all sources above a specified amount which has already been taxed by one of the scheduler taxes.

2.5.1 Business expenses

Business expenses may include those expenses that are directly incurred in earning income during a year. For example, proprietorship business, like any other types of business, incurs start-up expenses in order to initiate the business, and have to pay wages/salaries, interest, rent, and commodity and property taxes in order to carry out economic activities. They also incur other business expenses such as repair and maintenance expenses, advertisement expenses and legal or litigation fees. Other business expenses may include cost of trading stock disposed of during a tax year, doubtful accounts and bad debt written-off, depreciation and brought forward losses. These expenses are deemed necessary expenses and are the principal deductible expenses under the PIT system of EAC member countries.

Expenses like the cost of capital nature, domestic/personal expenses, fines, penalties, bribes, expenses incurred to generate exempt income or income subject to a final withholding tax, any additions to reserves that are not required by law, cost of goods purchased but subsequently returned to supplier or manufacturer, cost and expense of providing benefits for the owners, officers, and management that is not necessary for the conduct of business, non-qualifying bad debts, the distribution of profits, and PIT are not deductible.

2.5.2 Personal expenses

EAC countries commonly permit to deduct from gross income certain personal expenses such as contributions to provident funds, life insurance premiums and donations. For example, in Burundi, medical expenses incurred by a resident and his spouse and dependent children, and transport costs associated with a taxpayer, his wife and dependent children for a holiday destination once a year, are deductible. Burundi also allows up to 15% of the basic salary as commuting expenses in cases where an employee does not make use of employer provided transport.

In Tanzania, donations made to a charitable institution or social development project are deductible up to 2% of business income. Similarly, in Uganda donations up to 5% of the taxpayer's chargeable income are deductible.

2.6. Allowances/vanishing formula/tax credit

There is a practice to exempt an initial amount of income from tax by means of a basic allowance/zero-rate bracket, vanishing formula or tax credit. While under the basic allowance system, an initial amount of income is received free of tax by a taxpayer; under the vanishing formula system, the amount of basic allowance decreases and becomes zero after certain level of income. On the other hand, under the zero-rate-bracket system, a tax of zero percent applies to the initial amount of income below the tax bracket threshold, while a tax credit offsets the tax liability related to the initial amount of income.[9]

2.6.1 Basic allowance/zero-rate bracket

As mentioned above, while an initial amount of income is received free of tax under the basic allowance system, it is taxed at a zero-percent under the zero-rated bracket system. In the EAC region, there is a practice to zero-rate the initial amount of income below the tax bracket threshold. Since tax implication of basic allowance or zero-rate bracket system is the same, in this section, tax free initial amount will be known as basic allowance.

EAC countries provide basic and other allowances to individuals under their PITs. The basic allowance is simply a slice of initial amount of income received free of tax by every resident taxpayer. This means that resident taxpayers are allowed to deduct a certain amount of income from gross income before their PIT liability is calculated. Basic allowance is not provided to a non-resident taxpayer as he avails the facility in his home country.

The existing level of basic allowance in Burundi is BIF 1,800,000, Rwanda RWF 360,000, Tanzania TNZ 3,040,000 and Uganda UGX 2,820,000.

It is to be noted that a high level of basic allowances erodes the tax base, leading to a revenue loss. On the other hand, a low level of basic allowance would increase the number of taxpayers, thereby entailing, *inter alia*, administrative problems and, in addition, revenue benefits would probably be outweighed by other factors.

It is well known that a taxpayer's family circumstances can be taken into account under the PIT system. Because the taxpayer's ability to pay tax is affected by his/her family obligations, it is desirable to take into account family size while determining tax liability. Because a married man has to support his wife if his wife is not "gainfully employed," his level of basic allowance becomes lower than that of a single person and

---

9   OECD (2011). Special Features: Trends in Personal Income Tax and Employee Social Security Contribution Schedules. *Taxing Wages 2011*, Organisation for Economic Cooperation and Development, Paris, p.44. See http://www.oecd.org/tax/tax-policy/50131824.pdf.

is reduced further if he has dependent children or others. So there is a practice in some countries to provide spouse or dependent allowances under the PIT. They are, however, not common in the EAC region, where only Burundi allows a reduction of 5% of the amount of tax payable for each of the first four dependent members of a taxpayer's family up to 20%. The reduction, however, cannot exceed BIF 1,350 per dependent and no deduction is granted where taxable income exceeds BIF 300,000. Other EAC countries do not provide any allowance for spouse and dependents, which means the system of allowances of EAC countries is unfavourable for couples/families because it gives them less tax advantage by not giving any consideration for the cost of caring for spouse, children and elderly people.

On the other hand, a generous system of allowance where separate allowances are provided to spouse, children and elderly, tends to be costly in terms of revenue forgone. Further, some taxpayers might misuse the basic allowance system based on the number of children by creating artificial children. Besides, such a system tends to be more advantageous to the higher income groups than the lower ones because the higher income groups would be subject to lower marginal rates of tax due to generous exemptions than would be otherwise. These limitations of the basic allowance systems can be corrected to a great extent by adopting the vanishing formula.

2.6.2 Vanishing formula

As stated earlier, under the basic allowance system, higher income groups get more benefit than the lower income groups due to the applicability for lower marginal rate to high income. In response to this, some recommend the vanishing formula system. Under this system, the amount of basic allowance decreases and becomes zero after a certain level of income, meaning that the vanishing formula does not allow any exemption/benefit to taxpayers above a certain level of income. Thus only the lower income group obtains the full benefit of basic allowance.

Thus the vanishing formula system is more progressive than the system of basic allowance. Under this system, the basic allowance level could be increased for both equity and administrative reasons without much revenue loss. Thus the vanishing formula is justified on both equity and revenue grounds. It is, however, administratively complicated although tax tables can be prepared to reduce the magnitude of the problem. Further, the vanishing formula does not give good feeling to the higher income groups that do not get the advantage of the basic allowance. Due to these reasons the vanishing formula system has hardly been adopted by any country.

2.6.3 Tax credits

There is also a practice to provide tax credits instead of the basic allowance to relieve lower income groups from the burden of income taxation and/or to reduce their tax liability. Under the tax credit system, taxpayers receive a tax credit, i.e. a specified amount is deducted from a person's total tax liability rather than from his/her net income.[10] This system eliminates the difference in benefits among levels of income that exist under the basic allowance system. As stated earlier, under the basic allowance system, large income groups get more benefit due to the applicability for lower marginal rate to high income.

Since every taxpayer gets the same amount of relief irrespective of the level of income under the tax credit system, it eliminates the difference in benefits among levels of income that exist under the basic allowance system. The tax credit system is equitable since value of the tax credit, as proportion of income, is greater for the lower income group, while the dollar value of the credit is the same for all taxpayers. Every taxpayer gets the same amount of relief irrespective of the level of income. The re-distributional goal of the tax credit mechanism is achieved even more effectively under the non-wastable credits: "In case of a *wastable* (or non-refundable) tax credit, entitlements only accrue to the extent that they are off-set against tax liabilities, while *non-wastable* or refundable tax credits involve cash transfers to people (e.g. low income workers) whose tax liabilities are not large enough to make (full) use from a particular entitlement (tax credit)."[11]

Since the tax credit system simplifies tax administration, relieves lower income groups from the burden of taxation, improves equity, but at the same time enhances collection, it is becoming popular and several Organisation for Economic Cooperation and Development (OECD) countries have replaced tax allowances by tax credits in recent years.[12] Examples of countries that have adopted the tax credit system include Canada, the UK and the USA. In East Africa, only Kenya makes use of

---

10   For the example of Turkey, see *Tax News Service*, March 7, 2007.
11   OECD (2005). Note 4, "Tax/Benefit Policies and Parental Work and Care Decision" in *Babies and Bosses: Reconciling Work and Family Life*, Vol.4, ISBN 92-64-00928-0-0, Organization for Economic Cooperation Development, Paris, p.12.
12   OECD (2006). Tax Policy Studies, Fundamental Reform of Personal Income Tax No.13, Organization for Economic Cooperation and Development, Paris, p.62.

a tax credit mechanism in the form of personal relief where a resident individual can deduct KS 13,944 per annum from payable PIT.

2.7. Tax unit

Of the EAC countries, only Burundi has adopted a system of joint taxation. Under this system, the household is treated as a single tax unit and tax is levied on the joint income of a family. This means that income of the spouse and children is added to the income of the head of the family who has to file a tax return to the tax office. Such a system is adopted due to several factors. For example, traditionally, the husband has been considered the bread-winner and the wife, who is expected to take care of the family and to bring up the children while staying at home, is dependent on the husband. The income of the wife and children, if any, is treated as the income of her husband or father. As family is treated as the basic tax unit, husband and wife cannot claim the basic allowance separately.

Such a joint tax system is justified on the grounds that married couples could live more cheaply than two single adults due to the "economies of scale derived from living together,"[13] leading to an increase in tax paying capacity. Further, "spouses are to benefit...from the joy of each other's company"[14] who made joint decisions, *inter alia*, regarding their spending. So under the joint tax system, the income of all members of a family is aggregated and taxed jointly.

However, the joint taxation system has been replaced by the system of individual taxation over the years in some countries, including Kenya. Under the new system, an individual is the unit of taxation and the husband and wife are considered two separate individuals and are taxed separately. In Kenya, a married woman can file her own tax return and pay tax with respect of her professional/employment income, including dividends, interests and rental income. Rwanda also has adopted the system of individual taxation. When the tax liabilities of husband and wife are calculated separately, each of them is entitled to an individual basic allowance. This means that when couples are taxed separately, their income is subject to lower marginal rates, leading to a decline in their total tax bill. This is an incentive for secondary earners to take up paid employment. The system of individual taxation has also made

---

13   J.A. Kay & M.A. King, *The British Tax System*, Oxford University Press, Oxford, 1990, p.44.
14   *Ibid*, p.44.

withholding more simple and accurate since final tax liability depends only on the income of an individual.[15]

The system of individual taxation became more and more important over the years due to several reasons. Industrialisation and urbanisation have taken place in different EAC countries, leading to an increase in job opportunities. Expansion of the service sector in the EAC countries also has contributed to the job opportunities for females in this region. Consequently, the number of female workers in the labour market has been increasing year after year. Increase in the level of female education and changes in the social outlook further enhance women's participation in the work force. In modern society, more and more women prefer to take up a paid job rather than being simply a housewife and now females play a major role in the modern economy.

The practice of getting divorced has also been increasing. Under such a condition, the principle of marriage neutrality has attracted more attention than ever before. The marriage neutrality principle "implies that there should be no tax penalty for being married and none for being single."[16] Because the system of individual taxation is neutral regarding the marriage decision and also as it provides incentives for secondary earners, treatment of an individual as the tax unit is important under modern economies.

2.8. Tax rates

PIT is levied with progressive rates in all EAC countries. For the purpose of tax, taxable income is divided into several brackets. The first slice of income is exempt/subject to zero rate as basic allowance and the remaining income is taxed with progressively increasing rates. Kenya levies PIT with 5 rates (10%, 15%, 20%, 25% and 30%), while Tanzania 4 rates (i.e. 13%, 20%, 25% and 30%). On the other hand, Uganda levies PIT with four progressive rates ranging from 10% to 40% (10%, 20%, 30% and 40%). Burundi and Rwanda levy PIT with rates: 20% and 30%. PIT rates are given in Table 2.2.

15   Charles E. McLure, Jr., & Santiago Pardo R., "Improving the Administration of the Colombian Income Tax, 1986-88", in Richard M. Bird & Milka Casanegra de Jantscher, (editors.), *Improving Tax Administration in Developing Countries*, International Monetary Fund, Washington DC, 1992, p.141.

16   Robert Ngosa Simbyakula, "Zambia: Tax Treatment of the Family", *Bulletin for International Fiscal Documentation*, Vol. 44, October, 1990, p.524.

Table 2.2: PIT Rate Structure

Country	Taxable Income	Rate
Burundi	BIF	
	Up to 1,800,000	0%
	1, 8000,000 – 3,600,000	20%
	Over 3,600,000	30%
Kenya	KES	
	First 121,968	10%
	Next 114,912	15%
	Next 114,912	20%
	Next 114,912	25%
	Over 466,704	30%
Rwanda	RWF	
	Up to 360,000	0%
	360,001 – 1,200,000	20%
	Over 1,200,000	30%
Tanzania	TNZ	
	Up to 2,040,000	0%
	2,040,001-4,320,000	13%
	4,320,001-6,480,000	20%
	6,480,001-8,640,000	25%
	Over 8,640,000	30%
Uganda	UGX	
	Up to 2,820,000	0%
	2,820,001-4,020,000	10%
	4,020,001-4,920,000	20%
	4,920,001-12,000,000	30%
	Over 12,000,000	40%

A close look at the existing structure of PIT in the EAC countries indicates that while the number of rates is highest in Kenya, the (five) marginal rate is the highest in Uganda (40%). Both the level and number of PIT rates are not so high. Overall the existing structure of PIT in the EAC countries is reasonable.

2.9. Tax withholding

EAC countries collect PIT by means of a withholding mechanism on certain sources of income. They invariably levy withholding tax on wages/salaries. Withholding rates on wages/salaries are the same as PIT rates which are calculated on a prorate basis. They also levy withholding tax on other income payments such as interest, dividends, rents, and royalties. There is also a common practice to levy withholding tax on management, technical, or professional fees. EAC countries also levy withholding taxes on these sources of income generally with 10% to 20% rates.

In addition, different EAC countries levy withholding on different specific incomes. For example, in Tanzania payment for goods and services made by a corporation to persons other than holders of TIN is subject to withholding tax of 2% of gross payment in case of residents and 15% in case of non-residents. In Rwanda, performance payments made to professionals are subject to 15%, lottery or other gambling proceeds 15%, and public tenders 3%. In Uganda, contracts of goods and services exceeding UGX 1,000,000 are subject to 6% withholding tax.

In Kenya, performance payments made to professionals are subject to 20% in case of non-residents, pension/retirement annuity 10% to 30% for residents and 5% non-residents, shipping/aircraft business 2.5% in case of non-residents, contractual fees 3% in case of residents and 20% in case of non-residents, lease contract in the case of non-residents 15%, commission paid by insurance companies to brokers 5% in case of non-residents, commission paid by insurance companies to other than brokers 10%, commission paid to ticketing agents 5% in case of residents and transmitting message 5% in case of non-residents.

Some of the withholding taxes levied by EAC countries are final while others are non-final. For example, withholding taxes on interest and dividends are final while other withholding taxes are non-final in Uganda. Income[17] subject to final withholding tax is not added to other income of the taxpayer to assess PIT liability, no deduction is allowed for any expenditure or losses incurred in deriving incomes subject to final withholding tax and no credit or refund is allowed for the final withholding tax from the PIT liability. On the other hand, income subject to non-final withholding tax is added to total income and subject to general PIT; expenses or losses incurred in deriving non-final withholding tax are deductible and non-final withholding tax is treated

---

17   Management or professional fees, and payments made by government bodies, and local authorities are subject a non-final withholding tax of 6%.

as an advance tax which is credited against the final tax liability on total annual income, including income subject to non-final withholding tax of a taxpayer.

The withholding tax system is advantageous from several points of view. The system simplifies tax administration since tax is collected from relatively a small number of payers of income instead of a large number of receivers of income. Since a large number of taxpayers (i.e. employees, shareholders, depositors etc.) do not have to file tax returns, a withholding system minimises not only compliance costs but administrative costs as well. As the tax is collected from the employers, banks, companies etc. who are relatively organised and whose number is relatively smaller than that of employees, depositors and shareholders. The system helps minimise tax evasion. Further, a withholding system produces a steady flow of revenue to the exchequer.

However, withholding tax should not be levied on too many sources of income, particularly business income. As stated above, commercial imports and public tenders are subject to withholding tax in Rwanda and Uganda unless there is an explicit waiver, while Kenya levies withholding tax on shipping/aircraft business, contractual fees, lease contract, commission paid by the insurance companies to brokers and others, commission paid to ticketing agents and transmitting message. Such an extended system of withholding tax is prone to tax fraud by withholders since they might not deposit the withheld tax to the treasury. This system also creates difficulty to the taxpayers in getting credit for the amount withheld. The withheld tax paid on importation or purchases by the businessmen is most likely to be shifted forward to the consumers via higher prices. Under such a situation, the income tax system, in practice, operates like a turnover tax.

Instead of levying withholding tax on numerous payments, attempt must be made to make the payers of income liable to provide information. Where flow of income is documented, there is no need for withholding. It is, therefore, necessary to establish reporting requirement instead of withholding tax in the case of business income. Further, since an instalment payment system has been introduced under the PIT in various EAC countries, it would be better to make the instalment system effective to ensure that tax is collected. So follow-up on both reporting and instalment payments is preferred rather than levying withholding taxes on a variety of incomes. Withholding should be limited to income payment where the government is not sure that tax will be collected.

2.10. Presumptive tax

EAC countries levy presumptive tax on small business establishments, which are perceived either not to maintain records or the records are not up to an acceptable minimum standard. In the absence of required information, it becomes administratively difficult to determine net income by deducting allowable business expenses from gross income and to assess PIT. In such cases, attempts are made to levy tax not on net income but on some kind of rough measures of income. Presumptive taxes also can be levied with annual flat rates on certain types of income or taxpayers.

For example, in Rwanda small businesses with an annual turnover up to RWF 12 million are subject to a fixed tax as follows:

Annual Turnover (in RWF in million)
Between 2 and 4
Between 4 and 7
Between 7 and 10
Between 10 and 12

Uganda levies presumptive tax in the name of gross turnover tax in case of businesses whose annual turnover is between UGX 5 million and UGX 50 million. Kenya levies presumptive tax in the name of turnover tax at the rate of 3% of the annual gross sales. Similarly, a presumptive tax regime exists in Burundi in case of individuals whose annual turnover is below BFI 5 million if they provide service or accommodation, and BFI 10 million in case of others.

EAC countries have adopted presumptive tax on administrative grounds. It is levied in order to tap income which otherwise could not be tapped because the earners of such incomes are either outside of the income tax net or do not often file tax returns. There is, however, a problem with the general accuracy of the tax base which is fixed on the basis of criteria set by the tax administrators rather than on income declared by the taxpayers. This may also work as a hindrance to the development of sound business accounting practices, which is necessary to improve tax administration and tax compliance.

The presumptive tax should, therefore be levied only on those types of incomes or taxpayers that cannot be brought into the tax net otherwise. The presumptive rates may be kept fairly high so the taxpayers will be encouraged to come under the normal income tax regime.

2.11. Taxation of retirement saving

Generally, pensions and gratuity constitute retirement incomes. Pension is a stream of income paid over a period of time, while gratuity is a lump sum one-time payment. Sometimes employees receive income in other forms also such as a termination payment. Retirement saving may be taxed only once: either through having no deduction for contributions (payment made to a retirement fund for the provision or future provision of retirement payments), but then no tax on pension payments (retirement payments made to a retiree or his/her dependant in the event of a retiree's death), or by allowing deduction of contributions, but making all pension and gratuity income taxable.

There are different practices in the EAC regarding the taxation of retirement saving. For example, in Rwanda retirement contributions made to a qualified pension fund (maximum of 10% of employee's employment income or RWF 1,200,000/year, whichever is lower) is exempt from income tax. Besides, the income of qualified pension funds is exempt from income tax. On the other hand, pension payments are taxable. This means, retirement savings are exempt when they are put in to the qualified pension fund, they are exempt when they stay in the fund, but are taxable when they come out of the fund, which is known as an EET system, i.e. exempt, exempt and taxed.

However, the tax treatment of retirement savings associated with the state social security fund in Rwanda is slightly different, where not only contributions made by the employer on behalf of the employee to the state social security fund and the income of the State/Rwanda Social Security Fund are exempt, but also pension payments made under the state social security system are also exempt. This means such retirement savings escape income tax altogether, i.e. EEE (exempt, exempt and exempt).

On the other hand, in Uganda while contribution to a retirement fund and the income of retirement fund are not exempt, pension and lump sum payments made by a resident retirement fund to a member of the fund or his/her dependent in case of death of the member are exempt from income tax, i.e. TTE (taxed, taxed and exempt). In Kenya and Tanzania, while contributions made to an approved retirement fund are deductible, contributions to unapproved retirement fund are not deductible. On other hand, pension paid by both approved and unapproved resident retirement funds are exempt though the pension made by a non-resident fund is taxable. In Burundi, contributions up to 15% of basic salary are deductible and pensions are deductible.

2.12. Taxation of fringe benefits

Conceptually, since income received from whatever source or in whatever form provides the same benefit to its receiver, tax should be levied on all types of income in an equal manner. This also applies to fringe benefits, which are given by an employer to his employees in the form of automobile, rent free residential accommodation, utilities (telephone, electricity, and water), furniture, wages for domestic helpers, conveyance/transportation, education allowances, medical-insurance facilities, discounts, free meals, canteen facilities, entertainment allowances, holiday trips, gifts, vouchers or tokens, credit card and club expenses, interest free or concessional loans, employee stock options and tax paid by employers for employees. Exemption of fringe benefits from income tax distorts employment and compensation decisions as it encourages taxpayers to design a remuneration package where fringe benefits constitute a large part of remuneration to avoid income tax. Their exemption also narrows the tax base, complicates tax administration, and undermines the fairness of the tax system. So there is a need to levy tax on fringe benefits.

While tax on fringe benefits can be levied at the employee or employer level, it becomes difficult to levy income tax on fringe benefits at the recipient level as it requires handling of many specific situations. So it is desirable from an administrative point of view to levy a fringe benefit tax at the company level. This tax could be levied at a flat rate, say at the top individual income tax rate, on all fringe benefits including rent-free housing or motor vehicles, as it is done in Australia and New Zealand. The companies should get normal deduction of such taxed fringe benefits. Such a system would minimise the scope for manipulating the remuneration package by a company to lower the tax burden. Government will get revenue either in the form of a fringe benefit tax if a company decides to pay more fringe benefits than normal salary/wage or individual income tax if a company decides to pay higher wage/salary instead of fringe benefits.

There is, however, a limited use of fringe benefit tax at employers' level in the EAC countries. For example, Kenya levies a fringe benefit tax at employer level in respect of a loan provided at an interest rate lower than the market interest rate to an employee/director or his relatives. In general it is common in the EAC countries to include fringe benefits in gross salary of an employee and levy PIT. For example, in Rwanda benefits in kind received by an employee from an employer such as vehicles, accommodation and loans provided by an employer to his employee are included in the taxable income of an employee. In the case of office provided vehicle, 10% of the employment income is added to the taxable income. The corresponding figures are 20% for residential accommodation and 10% for loans. In Tanzania, while 10% of the employee's total annual income is added to the taxable income in case of employer provided free housing, the amount to be included in the taxable income in case of office provided vehicles is a specified amount based on engine size of the vehicle. In Uganda also different types of fringe benefits provided by an employer to the employees are included in the employee's taxable income. For example, in case the employer provides accommodation, the value of the benefit in kind is the lesser of:

- the market rent of the accommodation or housing reduced by any payment made by the employee for the benefit; or
- 15% of the annual employment income paid by the employer to the employee.

In Burundi free accommodation provided by the employer is presumed to be 10% of remuneration.

2.13. Taxation of dividends

While dividends in general are subject to withholding tax in the EAC countries, there are some variations in their taxation across the countries. For example, in Uganda, dividends paid to a resident shareholder are subject to a withholding tax of 10% when paid by a company listed on the stock exchange and at 15% when they are paid by other companies. In Tanzania, dividends distributed by a resident company are taxed in the form of a final withholding tax, while dividends distributed by a non-resident corporation are included in the shareholders income for tax purpose. In the case of resident companies, inter-corporate dividends are exempt from income tax in Tanzania, where the corporation receiving the dividend holds 25% or more of the shares in the corporation distributing the dividend and controls, either directly or indirectly, and 25% or more of the voting power in the corporation. On the other hand, in Rwanda, where dividend income includes income from shares and similar income distributed by companies, they are subject to withholding tax of 15%. The rate, however, is reduced to 5% on dividend income on securities listed on capital markets when the person who withholds is a resident taxpayer of Rwanda or of the EAC. In Burundi, dividend incomes are subject to PIT at the 15% by way of withholding tax. However, dividends distributed to shareholders of free-zone enterprises are exempt from tax. In Kenya, dividends are subject to a uniform rate of 15%.

2.14. Taxation of capital gains

In general, capital gain is the difference between the purchase price and the selling price of an asset,[18] which arises due to several reasons. For example, gains on land and buildings arise due to urbanisation, population increases, increase in economic activities and speculation, while gains on stock are the result of reinvestment of earnings by the corporations and/or increase in the earning capacity of a business due to improved management, development of new products and techniques, lessened competition etc.[19] Similarly, decline in the market rate of interest leads to an increase in bond price and sellers of bonds realise capital gains.

Further, gains also result from inflation. Such gains are, however, nominal gains, not real gains, that do not increase the command of individuals over commodities. This demands the adjustment of inflationary component of capital gains. While inflation adjustment for capital gains may be desirable it is difficult to implement. Even the simplest inflation adjustment system seems to be complicated for most EAC countries at this stage. Further, values of both asset and liabilities are affected by inflation.

Taxation of capital gains is advocated on various grounds such as equity, efficiency, revenue and stability. Since large part of capital gains is obtained by high income groups, capital gains taxation improves equity. Capital gains taxation also improves economic efficiency. This is because such a tax discourages investment in 'non-productive' assets such as land, buildings and antiques. Further, capital gains taxation also saves resources of both taxpayers and tax administration by not encouraging taxpayers to convert other incomes as capital gains and tax officers would not be required to initiate activities to check misclassification of income. If capital gains are exempt, taxpayers may try to classify other kinds of income as capital gains. Any attempts to

---

18   In general, land, buildings, capital equipment and securities are known as capital assets. Similarly, automobiles, jewellery, furniture, paintings, antiques and other consumer durables and intangible property like patent rights are also considered as capital assets. Capital assets are other than 'stock in trade'.

19   John F. Due, *Government Finance: An Economic Analysis*, Richard D. Irwin, Inc., Homewood, Illinois, 1963, p.180.

restrict the conversion of other income into capital gains would make the tax law and administration unnecessarily complex. For example, it becomes necessary to introduce several restrictions on the deductions of expenses and losses. Hence, taxation of capital gains is necessary to protect the income tax base though capital gain itself may not provide a large tax base. Capital gains tax helps maintain stability in the economy, as it plays a counter cyclical role since taxpayers have to pay more tax when the value of an asset appreciates and less when it depreciates.

Taxation of capital gains is not straightforward and there are different practices regarding capital gains tax around the world. For example, some countries impose corporate tax on the capital gains of the corporate taxpayers but a separate capital gains tax on the payers of PIT. Some counties include a wide range of assets in the tax base, while others exclude several types of assets from the tax net on various grounds, including political and administrative. Still some countries either exempt certain types of capital assets or adopt rollover provision, not to hinder the free flow of capital in the most productive uses. The taxation of capital gains has in fact been the most contentious issue in the field of income taxation.

There are different practices in the EAC countries regarding the tax treatment of capital gains. For example, in Rwanda, while capital gains resulting from sale or cession of commercial immovable property are taxed at 30%, capital gain on secondary market transactions on listed securities are exempt from capital gains tax. In Uganda, capital gains are included in the gross income of the taxpayer and assessed as a business income. In Burundi also there is no separate tax on capital gains, which are treated as ordinary income and are subject to the business tax. Capital gains are exempt from tax in Kenya except gains from sales on property shares in respect of oil/mining/mineral prospecting companies that is taxed at 10%. In Tanzania, while gains on depreciable assets are included in the income of an individual and subject to normal PIT rates, gains on non-depreciable assets are subject to a 10% capital gains tax.

2.15 Summary

In the EAC region, PIT is imposed on the taxable income received for the provision of labour or capital or both in the form of employment income, business income and investment/property income. The tax is basically levied on the worldwide income of a resident taxpayer, but only on the income from domestic source in the case of a non-resident taxpayer. In general, income received by a taxpayer from various sources is added together which is subject to progressive tax rates though some sources are subject to separate taxes. Withholding taxes and presumptive taxes are also commonly used by EAC countries.

PIT is levied on net income, which is obtained by deducting from the gross income business expenses and personal expenses. Besides, an initial amount of income is exempt from tax by means of a basic allowance/zero-rate bracket in all the EAC countries, except Kenya which provides a tax credit. PIT is levied with progressive rates in all EAC countries and both the level and number of tax rates also is in line with the modern international common practice as the top marginal rate is 40% in Uganda and the highest number of rates is 5 in Kenya. EAC member states also make use of withholding taxes and presumptive taxes. They also levy PIT in some ways on fringe benefits, retirement saving, dividends and capital gains.

Appendix 2 (a): Withholding Tax Rates in Tanzania

Description of Payment	Rate for Resident	Rate for Non Resident
(i) Dividends from the Dar es Salaam Stock Exchange listed corporations		
(ii) Dividend from resident corporation	5%	5%
to another resident corporation where the corporation receiving the dividend holds 25% or more of the shares in the corporation	5%	NA
Dividends from other corporations	10%	10%
Interest	10%	10%
Royalties	15%	15%
Other Withholding payments from Investment Returns.	15%	15%

Description of Payment	Rate for Resident	Rate for Non Resident
Rental Income	10%	15%
Technical services fees (mining)	5%	15%
Transport (Non-resident operator/charterer without permanent establishment).	NA	5%
Insurance Premium	0%	5%
Natural Resources Payment	15%	15%
Service Fees	5%	15%
Directors Fee (Non full time Directors)	15%	15%
Commission to agents by service providers on money transfer through mobile phones	10%	10%
Payments for goods supplied to Government and its institutions by any person	2% of gross payment	N/A

Source: http://www.tra.go.tz/index.php/withholding-tax

Chapter 3

Business Profit Tax

3.1. Introduction

EAC partner states levy tax on the income of companies (legal entities). The tax is levied under the General Tax Code[1] in Burundi, Income Tax Act 1974 in Kenya, Laws on Direct Taxes on Income 2005 in Rwanda, the Income Tax Act 2004 in Tanzania and the Income Tax Act 1997 in Uganda. Taxes levied on the income of companies are simply called income taxes in Kenya, Tanzania, and Uganda, tax on business income in Burundi, and corporate income tax in Rwanda. In this chapter, tax levied on the income of companies is referred to as business profit tax (BPT).

In Rwanda, BPT is levied on companies, cooperative societies, public business enterprises, partnerships, and de facto companies or associations and any other entities that perform business activities, and are established to realise profits. In Tanzania, BPT is levied on the profits of a corporation, where the term "corporation" is defined broadly to include, among others, companies, corporate bodies, and

---

1   As contained in the Government of Burundi Law of 21 September 1963, and as amended to date.

associations or other bodies of persons. The tax is also levied on the income of a trust/unit trust. In Uganda, BPT is levied on companies where the term "company" means a body of persons, corporate or unincorporated, whether created or recognised under the law in force in Uganda or elsewhere, and a unit trust, but does not include any other trusts or partnerships. In Burundi, BPT payers include: public limited companies, private limited liability companies, private companies, single-owner limited liability companies, civil companies, joint ventures and cooperative societies.

There are different practices regarding the application of the BPT to partnerships.[2] For example, in Rwanda, a partnership is taxed on its own income at the BPT rate, not on behalf of its partners, who are not taxed again on the income they receive from the partnership. On the other hand, partnerships are not subject to BPT in Tanzania, where incomes or losses of partnerships are treated as incomes or losses of their partners and are taxed at the individual level. In Uganda, a partnership is required to file a return but the profit of a partnership is distributed among the partners and taxed at their hands.

3.2. Exemptions

EAC member countries have exempted many organisations from BPT. Major exemptions provided in these countries are summarised in Table 3.1.

Table 3.1: Major Exemptions Granted Under the EAC BPTs

Country	Major Exemptions under BPT
Burundi	State, municipalities and public bodies
	Companies exempt under the investment code
	Free zone enterprises
	Agricultural and stock-breeding enterprises
	Passenger buses and minibuses operating companies

---

2   Partnerships fall in the borderline area, i.e. the profit of a partnership can either be taxed at the level of partnership under the BPT or it can be divided among the partners; in the latter case, each partner's share is added to the partner's other income and subject to PIT. Ideally, the distributable/distributed earnings of a partnership should be taxed at the partner's level together with the partner's other income, but the practice in some countries is to consider the income of a partnership as arising to the partnership and subject to BPT.

Country	Major Exemptions under BPT
Kenya	Profits or gains of an agricultural society
	Income of a local authority
	Income of an institution, body of persons, or irrevocable trust of a public character established solely for the purposes of the relief of poverty or distress of the public, or for the advancement of religion or education
	Income of a registered pension scheme, trust scheme, pension fund, provident fund, retirement fund, and National Social Security Fund
	Income of a registered home ownership savings plan
	Income from the investment of an annuity fund, or an insurance company
Rwanda	The Rwanda Development Bank
	Entities that carry on only activities of a religious, humanitarian, charitable, scientific or educational character, unless the revenue received during a tax period exceeds the corresponding expenses to the extent that those entities conduct a business
	The Rwanda Social Security Fund and qualified pension funds
Tanzania	The Price Stabilisation and Agricultural Inputs Trust
	The Investor Compensation Fund
	Farmers' cooperative society
Uganda	Income of listed institutions, income of any local authority
	Interest earned by a financial institution on a loan granted to pay persons for the purpose of farming, forestry, bee keeping, animal and poultry husbandry or similar operations

Other commonly exempt organisations in the EAC region include national, state and local governments, central banks, the East African Development Bank, and organisations covered by a bilateral agreement, or an international treaty to which an EAC member country is a party.

3.3. Income

BPT is levied on net income or profit of legal entities, which is calculated by deducting allowable business expenses from the gross income. Income can be from domestic as well as foreign source income. Tax treatment of foreign source income in the EAC region depends in general upon whether a taxpayer is resident or non-resident in the country concerned.

Resident and non-resident companies are distinguished mainly on the basis of the place of incorporation or location of effective management/control. For example, in Uganda, a resident company is defined as a company that is incorporated or formed under the law of Uganda, or its management and control has been exercised in Uganda at any time during the income year, or it undertook the majority of its operations in Uganda during the income year. Similarly, in Kenya, a resident company is defined as a company incorporated under a law of Kenya or the management and control of the affairs was exercised in Kenya or it is declared by the Finance Minister by notice in the Gazette to be resident in Kenya. In Burundi, resident companies are defined as those companies that are incorporated under the law applicable in Burundi, and the head office is located in Burundi.

Rwanda also has taken similar approach. A company is considered as resident in Rwanda if it is established according to Rwandan laws, or its place of effective management is located in Rwanda or it is a Rwanda government company. Almost similar definition exists in Tanzania, where a company is a resident if it is incorporated or formed under the Tanzanian laws or at any time during the income year, the management and control of the company were exercised in Tanzania. Other companies, that are not resident companies, are non-resident companies for the purpose of BPT in these countries.

While in Burundi the tax is levied only on Burundi source income in case of all companies, whether resident[3] or non-resident, in other EAC countries, resident companies are taxed on their worldwide income and non-resident companies on domestic source income only.

3.4. Deductible business expenses

BPT is levied on profit, which is obtained by deducting business expenses incurred in generating taxable income, from the gross income. Business expenses may include start-up expenses, cost of trading stock disposed of during the tax year, wages/salaries, rent, repair and maintenance expenses, advertising costs, head office expenses, taxes other than income taxes, social security contributions, insurance premiums, legal or litigation fees, doubtful accounts and bad debts written off, depreciation and losses brought forward.

In the EAC region, Burundi has adopted an itemised system of deduction, where the deductible items are specifically mentioned in the tax law and no deduction is allowed for any other items. Such a system ensures uniform treatment of all taxpayers, particularly in countries

---

3   However, foreign source dividends, interests and royalties of a resident company are
        subject to BPT in Burundi.

where the tax administration is young and weak, and the accounting system is not well developed. On the other hand, this method suffers from several limitations. For example, it is not possible to envisage an extensive list of the possible expenses in some types of businesses such as information technology, where there might be a need to spend on new items over a period of time. If such items are not included in the list of deductible items, they cannot be deducted. On the other hand, some businesses may misclassify those expenses that are not included in the list of deductible expenses in order to claim them as deductible expenses. This means that businesses that do not misclassify the expenses may be discriminated against.

In the backdrop of this, there is a tendency among countries to adopt a general system of deduction in place of the itemised system, where all business expenses incurred during the tax period, wholly and exclusively in connection with economic activities, are deductible. This is true in all the EAC member countries except Burundi. These countries do not specify in the tax laws business expense that is deductible for the calculation of BPT. Rather, they allow taxpayers to deduct all the business expenses incurred directly in earning the business income in the income year. For example, in Rwanda business expenses are deductible when:

- they are incurred for the direct purpose of, and in the normal course of the business;
- they correspond to a real expense and can be substantiated with proper documents;
- they lead to a decrease in the net assets of the business; and
- they are used for activities related to the tax period in which they are incurred.

Similarly, in Tanzania all items of expenditure incurred during the income year by a company, wholly and exclusively in the production of taxable income, are deductible. It is also true in Uganda where all expenditures and losses incurred in the production of income included in gross income during the income year are deductible.

EAC countries, however, do specify some expenses even under the general deduction system. In case of some expenses they also fix maximum deductible limits for policy reasons or to protect the revenue. For example, commonly specified expenses in the tax laws of the EAC countries include costs for repairs and improvements, pollution control, research and development, advertising, donations, bad debts and provisioning, which are briefly outlined below.

3.4.1 Pre-operation expenses:

Pre-operating expenses may include expenses for the preparation of a feasibility study or project document, registration of a company, legal advice, printing, conducting market surveys and trial production activities. In countries like Uganda, the cost of starting a business is deductible in equal instalments over a period of four years during the operation of the business.

3.4.2 Trading stock:

EAC countries also allow deduction of trading stock. For example, in Tanzania, deductible allowance in respect of the trading stock of a business is calculated as follows:
- the opening value of trading stock of the business for the income year,
- *plus* expenditure incurred by the person during the income year that is included in the cost of trading stock of the business,
- *less* the closing value of trading stock of the business for the income year.

3.4.3 Repair and maintenance expenses:

In some EAC countries, repair and maintenance expenses are deductible in the year they are incurred. Such expenses are necessary in order to prevent a decline in the value of assets. For example, in Tanzania, while all expenditures incurred in respect of the repair or maintenance of depreciable assets owned and employed by the company wholly and exclusively in the production of income from the business are deductible, no deduction is allowed for expenditure in improving an asset. In Uganda, a taxpayer is allowed a deduction for expenditure incurred during the income year for the repair of property occupied or used by the business in the production of taxable income.

3.4.4 Training, research and development expenses:

These expenses are also deductible. For example, in Rwanda, all training and research expenses that promote activities during a tax period are deductible. In Uganda, a person is allowed a deduction for scientific research expenditure incurred during the income year in the course of conducting a business, income from which is included in gross income.

3.4.5 Advertising expenses:

In the EAC countries advertisement expenses are deductible fully or partially. For example, in Kenya, expenditure on advertising in connection with a business, to the extent that the Commissioner considers just and reasonable, are deductible. In Burundi, representation cost up to 1% of turnover, but not exceeding BIF 200,000, is deductible.

3.4 6 Donations:

Though donations do not relate directly to the acquisition of income, donations to specified activities which need to be promoted are fully deductible in some countries, but other countries impose limits in terms of a maximum amount or as a percentage of the total turnover or net income. They are deductible in the EAC countries, but there are different practices regarding the deductibility of donations. For example, in Uganda, the amount of deductible donations in a year cannot be more than 5% of the taxpayer's chargeable income. In Burundi, donations up to 1% of turnover but not more than 1% of net profit from previous year are deductible. In Tanzania, donations made to a charitable institution or social development project are deductible up to 2% of business income.

3.4.7 Reserves/provisions:

Banks and insurance companies are commonly allowed to deduct reserves from current income. This is because financial businesses are more risky, more unpredictable and more uncertain than other business. Instability in the financial sector may destabilise the whole economy. That is why central banks and insurance boards establish specific prudential standards, such as provisioning, which need to be maintained to meet future costs and liabilities. Reserves that are required by the governing laws are deductible for purposes of BPT assessment. Such provisions can be misused, however, if taxpayers use them to postpone tax payments. That is why the income tax laws of some countries set limits on the deductibility of reserves, meaning that tax accounting rules may not recognise all financial rules.

Tax laws of the EAC countries contain some special rules for banking and insurance sectors because of their special nature. For example, in Rwanda, in the determination of business profit, commercial banks and leasing entities are allowed to deduct any increase of the mandatory reserve for non-performing loans, as required by the directives of the National Bank of Rwanda related to management of bank loans and similar institutions. Business profit is increased by the entire amount recovered from bad debts deducted from such reserves. In Burundi, an amount up to 20%, 40% and 100% is deductible for the debts due for more than 6 months, 9 months and 12 months, respectively.

3.4.8 Bad debts:

Bad debts are deductible if specified conditions are met. For example, in Rwanda, bad debts may be deducted in a tax year if the following conditions are satisfied:
- if an amount corresponding to the debt was previously included in the income of the taxpayer;
- if the debt is written off in the books of accounts of the taxpayer; and
- if the taxpayer has taken all possible steps in pursuing payment and has shown concrete proofs that the debtor is insolvent.

In Uganda, a taxpayer is allowed a deduction for the amount of a bad debt written off in his accounts during the income year if the amount of the debt claim was included in the person's gross income in any year of income, or if the amount of the debt claim was in respect of money lent in the ordinary course of a business carried on by a financial institution in the production of income included in gross income.

3.4.9 Interest:

There are different practices regarding the deductibility of interest in the EAC countries. For example, in Uganda, a business is allowed to deduct interest incurred during the income year with respect of a debt obligation to the extent that the debt obligation has been incurred by the business in the production of income included in gross income. In Kenya, interest paid on loans used wholly and exclusively in the production of investment income in the tax year is deductible. This is also the case in Burundi where interest paid on loans used in the running of the business is deductible.

Tanzania has introduced thin capitalisation rules to protect the tax base where the total amount of interest that an exempt-controlled resident entity may deduct for a year of income should not exceed the sum of:
- all interest derived by the entity during the year of income that is to be included in calculating the entity's total income for the income year,

- *plus* 70 percent of the entity's total income for the income year calculated without including any interest derived or deducting any interest incurred by the entity.

Any interest for which a deduction is denied may be carried forward and treated as incurred during the next income year.

These thin capitalisation rules are intended to protect the tax base by reducing the possibility for avoiding tax through debt financing rather than equity financing by exempt-controlled resident entities.

3.5. Non-deductible expenses

Expenses that are not made for preserving or enhancing taxable transactions are not deductible. For example, domestic/personal expenses are not deductible as they are not connected with business. Similarly, fines, penalties, and bribes are also disallowed. This is because fines and penalties are paid for non-compliance with the law, not for the furtherance of business. From a public policy point of view, bribes are non-deductible because the deterrent effect will be diminished if they are deductible. Non-deductible expenses specified in the income tax laws of the EAC countries are summarised below:

Table 3.2: Non-deductible Expenses in the EAC Countries

Country	Non-deductible expenses
Burundi	Taxes on income
	Mortgage interest on buildings rented out
	Real estate tax to the extent that it is not a business expense
	Directors' fees and other amounts paid to Directors of joint-stock companies
	Fines of any kind
Kenya	Expenditure or loss which is not wholly and exclusively incurred in the production of income
	Capital expenditure
	Personal consumption expenses
	Income tax
	Sums contributed to a registered or unregistered pension, savings, or provident scheme or fund
	A premium paid under an annuity contract

Country	Non-deductible expenses
Rwanda	Reserve allowances, savings and other special-purpose funds, unless otherwise provided for by the income tax law
	Fines and similar penalties
	Donations and gifts exceeding 1% of turnover as well as donations given to profit making persons irrespective of the amount
	Income tax paid in accordance with the income tax law or paid abroad on business profit, and recoverable VAT
	Personal consumption expenses
	Entertainment expenses
	Expenses incurred on re-valuation of assets and related depreciation
	Expenses paid on business overheads, as in the case of telephone, electricity and fuel, whose use cannot be practically separable from private or non-business
Tanzania	Consumption expenditure
	Capital expenditure that secures a benefit lasting longer than twelve months or incurred in respect of natural resource prospecting, exploration and development
	Excluded expenditure: (a) income tax; (b) bribes and expenditure incurred in corrupt practice; (c) fines and similar penalties payable to a government or a political subdivision of a government of any country for breach of any law or subsidiary legislation; (d) expenditure to the extent to which incurred by a person in deriving exempt amounts or final withholding payments; or (e) distributions by an entity
Uganda	Domestic/private expenses
	Expenses of capital nature
	Expenses recoverable under any insurance contract, indemnity
	Income tax
	Reserve fund
	Gift, not included in recipient individual income
	Fine/penalty
	Contribution to retirement fund
	Life insurance premium
	Pension

The cost of a capital nature is also not deductible since assets are used to generate income for more than one year. Instead, the depreciation on capital assets may be deducted during the useful life of the assets. On the other hand, neither the cost of acquisition and/or improvement of land are deductible nor deprecation allowed as value of land does not decrease with its use and the useful life is not fixed.

Similarly, expenses incurred to generate exempt income or income subject to a final withholding tax are also not deductible as these incomes are not included in the taxable income. Donations (except authorised donations) are not deductible as well. Non-qualifying bad debts are not deductible. All these expenses are also not incurred to preserve or enhance taxable profits.

The distribution of profits may not be treated as an expense; the profits are the results of the business. Non-deductible profits include profits distributed as dividends and profits transferred to reserves. Similarly, BPT is not deductible in computing net income. This is because this tax is levied on net income, which is obtained after all deductions are made. Similarly, VAT, for which the taxpayer has claimed a rebate or credit for input tax is not deductible.

Other examples of non-deductible expenses may include: any additions to reserves that are not required by law, cost of goods purchased but subsequently returned to supplier or manufacturer, cost of goods purchased but used by the owners or employees for personal or household purposes and not sold, cost and expense of providing benefits for the owners, officers, and management that are not necessary for the conduct of business.

3.6. Depreciation

As stated earlier, costs of a capital nature are not deductible in computing taxable income for the purpose of BPT. These costs are incurred to buy assets that have a useful life of more than one year. Capital assets may be tangible and intangible. Tangible assets include machinery, equipment, vehicles, furniture, buildings and land, whereas intangible assets include patents, trademarks, copyrights and business goodwill.

Capital assets are used to generate income for several years. Their value decreases over time due to wear and tear. This loss in value is deductible in computing taxable income over the useful life of an asset. Thus, the cost of an asset is spread over the time it is used.[4] A full deduction of capital costs in the year of purchase would lead to understating taxable income in the year of purchase and overstating income in the following years when the capital assets are used. Therefore, instead of a

---

4   It is to be noted that in some countries, the taxes, fees and revenue stamps paid on the acquisition of capital assets may be added to their cost, capitalised and depreciated. Similarly, there is also a practice around the world to capitalise and amortise legal and litigation fees. For example, the legal fees for negotiating a long-term lease are capitalised and depreciated, as are the costs of improving an asset.

full deduction for the cost of capital assets, capital assets used to derive taxable income are depreciated over their useful life.

It must, however, be remembered that to be depreciable, an asset must have a limited useful life that can be estimated with reasonable accuracy. If it is not possible to establish the useful life of an asset, depreciation is not allowed. For example, in Rwanda, land, fine art, antiquities, jewellery, and any other assets that are not subject to wear and tear or obsolescence and do not have fixed useful life, are not depreciated.

In theory, businesses should be allowed to deduct the cost of an asset according to its wear and tear each year, but this is not possible for practical reasons. That is why some methods have been developed to calculate the depreciation of an asset which is in fact a notional expense. The depreciation rates are based on the estimated useful life of an asset.[5] The rates may be set by the government and provided in the income tax regulations. Alternatively, the government may set only the normative rates, and taxpayers themselves set the depreciation rates. If the depreciation rates are too low, they constrain capital investment and impede cash flow. On the other hand, high rates decrease tax liability. Attempts may be made to set the depreciation rates in such a way that the depreciation allowances approximate as closely as possible the annual loss in the value of a depreciable asset.

Of the EAC countries, Burundi has adopted an itemised system of depreciation, where depreciable items are listed separately and depreciation rates are specified for each item in the tax law. Kenya also has adopted the itemised system of depreciation. On the other hand, in other EAC countries, there is a common practice to adopt a pooled system of depreciation.[6] There is also a practice to adopt an itemised system of deprecation in case of some assets and a pooled system in case of others. For example, Rwanda has adopted an itemised system in case

---

5   The useful life of a depreciable asset is generally specified in the tax law. If the useful life is deemed to be too short, the result is a tax deferral, and vice versa. In addition, generous depreciation rates lead to a tax deferral; the opposite is true if the rates are very conservative.

6   While the useful life and depreciation rate for each asset are given separately under the itemised system, all assets of a similar nature are put into a group and treated as a single asset for depreciation purposes under the pooled system. Under the pooled system, the purchase price of an asset is added to the sum in the appropriate pool, and the sale price of an asset is subtracted from the sum in the appropriate pool. The pooled system is administratively simple because the depreciable assets are grouped in a few (e.g. four or five) classes and the depreciation rates are fixed for each class. Since depreciation is a notional expense, on administrative grounds, it is better to classify assets in a few categories, but oversimplification may penalise assets with a shorter life vis-à-vis their counterparts with a longer life.

of buildings and intangible assets, where the rate of deprecation in case of building is 5% of the cost price, while it is 10% of the cost price in case of non-tangible assets. This is also true in Uganda which has adopted an itemised system of deprecation in case of industrial buildings with 5% depreciation rate.

Rwanda and Uganda have adopted a pooled system of deprecation in case of other assets. Rwanda has classified other depreciable items in two broad categories. Uganda has classified them into four groups.

Table 3.3: Depreciation Rates in Selected EAC Countries

Pool	Assets	Rate
Rwanda		
A	Computers and accessories, information and communication systems, software products and data equipment	50%
B	All other business assets	25%
Uganda		
1	Computers and data handling equipment	40%
2	Automobiles; buses and mini-buses with a seating capacity of less than 30 passengers; goods vehicles with a load capacity of less than 7 tons; construction and earth moving equipment	35%
3	Buses with a seating capacity of 30 or more passengers; goods vehicles designed to carry or pull loads of 7 tons or more; specialised trucks; tractors; trailers and trailer-mounted containers; plant and machinery used in farming, manufacturing or mining operations	30%
4	Rail cars, locomotives and equipment; vessels, barges, tugs and similar water transportation equipment; aircraft; specialised public utility plant, equipment and machinery; office furniture, fixtures and equipment; any depreciable asset not included in another class.	20%

On the other hand, Tanzania has adopted a purely pooled system of depreciation where depreciable assets are divided into 8 categories and separate depreciation rates are fixed for each category ranging from 5% to 100%, depending upon the nature of assets included in each pool.

EAC countries also are diverse in case of selection of depreciation methods. Some countries have adopted the declining balance method,[7] while others the straight-line method.[8] Still some countries have adopted one method in case of one type of assets and another method in case of others. For example, Uganda has adopted the straight-line method in case of building and the diminishing/declining balance method in case of other assets. Tanzania has adopted the diminishing value method in case of several assets, including computers, vehicles and office furniture, and the straight-line method in case of buildings, and intangible assets. While in general Burundi has adopted the straight-line method, some assets such as hardware and software are subject to the declining balance method. These methods may best be explained with the help of numerical examples as follows:

Let us begin with the straight-line method that applies to building where the depreciation basis is the acquisition value of the asset. Let us also suppose the rate of deprecation is 10% and the purchase price of a building is USD 50,000. The taxpayer can claim depreciation expense of USD 5,000 each year from year 1 to year 10 as follows:

Table 3.4: Calculation of Depreciation under the Straight-Line Method

Year	Straight-Line Method 10%	
	Annual Depreciation	Year End-Book Value
1	5,000	45,000
2	5,000	40,000
3	5,000	35,000
4	5,000	30,000
5	5,000	25,000
6	5,000	20,000
7	5,000	15,000
8	5,000	10,000
9	5,000	5,000

7   Under the declining-balance method, the depreciation rate is applied to the written-down value of an asset or the class of asset, and the allowance gradually decreases over the years. The declining-balance method recognises that assets depreciate more in the early years of their useful life.

8   Under the straight-line method, the rate of depreciation is applied to the original value of an asset or class of asset and an equal allowance is provided for a number of years. The straight-line method assumes that assets depreciate by an equal percentage of the original value during their useful life.

Year	Straight-Line Method 10%	
10	5,000	0
Total Depreciation		USD 50,000

While the depreciation basis for assets is the acquisition value, the declining balance method of depreciation applies the depreciation rate to the ending balance of the group. The ending balance of the group is the beginning balance of the group in the following tax year. The balance of a category for purposes of calculating depreciation deduction in any taxable period is the amount determined as follows:

- the balance of the category at the end of the preceding year,
- _plus_ purchases of property in that category,
- _minus_ the amount received from the sale of property in that category.

Under the declining balance method, depreciation is calculated as follows:

Let us suppose ABC Company was set up in 2010 and its purchase and sales of assets were as follows and depreciation rate is 25%:

Year	Purchases	Sales
2010	40,000	0
2011	20,000	0
2012	30,000	0
2013	0	20,000
2014	0	12,000

In this case, depreciation may be calculated as follows:

Table 3.5: Calculation of Depreciation under the Declining Balance Method

Year	Beginning balance	Purchases	Sales	Balance before depreciation	Amount of depreciation deduction at 25%	Ending balance
2010	0	40,000	0	40,000	10000	30,000
2011	30,000	20,000	0	50,000	12,500	37,500
2012	37,500	0	0	37,500	9,375	28,125
2013	28,125	30,000	0	58,125	14,431	43,694
2014	43,594	0	20,000	23,594	5,898	17,696
2015	17,695	0	0	17,695	4,424	13,271

Year	Beginning balance	Purchases	Sales	Balance before depreciation	Amount of depreciation deduction at 25%	Ending balance
2016	13,271	0	12,000	1,271	318	953

In 2017, the company can deduct the entire amount of USD 953 as business expense since it is less than USD 1,000. This is common under the deprecation system adopted in the EAC region. For example, the entire depreciation basis is deductible as business expense if it does not exceed RWF 500,000 in Rwanda and TZS 1,000,000 in Tanzania. If the depreciation basis is less than zero, that amount is added to the profit of the business and thereafter the deprecation basis becomes zero.

Depreciation allowances may be taken when assets are used in a business, but not as soon as they are purchased.[9] From an administrative point of view, it is easier to treat an asset as being used from the middle of the year on the assumption that about half the assets are purchased in the first half of the year and the remaining in the second half. This means that a business may claim one half of the first year's depreciation irrespective of the time the asset was used. This policy might, however, encourage a business to buy and put in use assets at the end of the income year.[10]

3.7. Treatment of business losses

Sometimes, a business might incur losses, where the expenses of a company are higher than the revenue. This might happen under such situations as in the case of newly established industries where the gestation period is high, when there is large inventory build-up, when prices in the market fall due to lack of demand etc.

---

9   In case of leased assets, depreciation is allowed to the lessee in case of finance lease and to the lessor in case of operating lease (Rwanda, for example).

10   Some countries provide special depreciation allowances for plant and machinery used in double or triple shifts because they result in high wear and tear. This system may encourage high utilisation of assets, but it invites administrative complications. In addition, some special depreciation methods (e.g. accelerated depreciation) have been adopted to achieve certain policy objectives. Accelerated depreciation allows taxpayers to depreciate an asset in the early years of its useful life at a higher rate than is justified on purely technical or economic grounds. Accelerated depreciation means postponing tax in proportion to the investment made by the company concerned. This allows companies to use money in other areas for a certain period. It is said that "... an immediate, instead of a phased, reduction would exert a psychological impact on the investors." See Sri Lanka, Government of. Report of the Taxation Commission, Government Publications Bureau, Colombo, 1991, p.132.

Business losses can be set off against the profit from any or only specified sources of income in the future or past years. For example, business loss, whether domestic or foreign, can be offset against income from any income source whether domestic or foreign. Or, a foreign source loss can be offset against only foreign source income. Similarly, investment loss can be offset against only investment income. Loss can be set off with the income of the future years or past years. There are different practices in the EAC countries regarding the treatment of business losses. For example, countries like Rwanda, Uganda and Tanzania have adopted quarantine rules with different degrees of limitation. In Rwanda, foreign sourced losses cannot be offset against current or future domestic sourced business profit. In Uganda, farming loss can be set off only against farming income in the following year. Tanzania has adopted very detailed quarantine rules as follows:

- Losses incurred in a domestic business are deductible against all types of income from any source (domestic or foreign);
- Losses from a domestic investment may be deducted only against investment income, whether domestic or foreign;
- Foreign losses may be offset only against foreign income;
- Of the foreign losses, business losses may be offset against foreign business or investment income, but losses from a foreign investment may be offset only against foreign investment income.
- Losses incurred from agricultural business may be offset only against income from agricultural business.

All the EAC countries allow taxpayers to carry over losses and offset them against profits in future years. For example, losses can be carried forward for five years in Burundi (six years in case of exploration and research activities) and in Rwanda. Rwanda allows carry back loss to the long term contract on its completion, which means a long-term contract business can offset its loss against previously taxed business profit from that contract to the extent it cannot be absorbed by business profit in the tax period of completion.[11]

---

11   Government of Rwanda. Article 20 of Law No. 16/2005 of 18/08/2005 on Direct Taxes on Income.

Loss carry-back provision is generally advocated in case of more risky sectors, e.g. the financial sector, and to long-term global contracts. From taxpayers' point of view, a loss carry-back is more beneficial than a loss carry-forward because under the former system taxpayers' loss is adjusted immediately, while under the latter system taxpayers can adjust their losses in future. Due to the inflation, the present value of losses deducted in the future is less than the value of losses used currently, but taxpayers are not paid interest on the amount of a loss carry-forward. Loss carry-backs, however, have both revenue and administrative implications as it is necessary to make adjustment of current year's loss with previous year's income and make refunds to the taxpayers. So the use of carry-back may be restricted.

As a conservative treatment of losses is biased against new businesses with a long gestation period as well as risky businesses whose income is likely to fluctuate significantly, it tends to discourage risk-taking and inhibit economic growth. On the other hand, a liberal system for loss set-offs, where taxpayers are allowed to deduct losses from any source of income and carry losses backward or forward for a relatively long period, would "neutralize the impact of the tax on an investor's choice between the more and the less risky investment."[12] It is, therefore, desirable to adopt liberal rules for the tax treatment of losses and thus make the tax system growth-oriented.

3.8. Tax rates

Unlike PIT, which is commonly levied with progressive rates, BPT is generally levied at a flat rate due to several reasons. For example, a flat rate is desirable from an efficiency point of view as it does not penalise efficient companies that generate more profit. On the other hand, a progressive rate structure may penalise an efficient company as it has to pay more tax than an inefficient company that generates little profit. Besides, an efficient company may be tempted to show more expenses and less profit in its accounts in order to lower its tax liability. Progressive rates also may encourage a large company to split up into smaller ones, not for economic reasons, but to lower its tax liability, leading to both a revenue loss and economic distortion. Further, there is no justification for a progressive rate structure in a BPT system as there is in a PIT system on equity grounds because companies are simply a "conduit"

---

12   Malcolm Gillis (edit.), *Fiscal Reforms for Columbia* (Richard A. Musgrave Commission Report), The Law School of Harvard University, Cambridge, 1971, p.84.

through which income flows to individuals, who are the ultimate owners.[13] The size of a company is not significant from the point of view of taxable capacity because, although a small company may have fewer shareholders than a large company, the taxable capacity of the shareholders of both types of companies may be similar.[14] A priori, one cannot say that the taxable capacity of the shareholders of a large company is higher than that of the shareholders of a small company. It is safe to say that shareholders who fall in different income groups own companies.[15]

Because of the above mentioned reasons, BPT is levied around the world at a flat rate. There has been a trend around the world to reduce the BPT rate and the tax is being levied at much lower rates now than it used to be until the early 1980s.[16] EAC countries have also largely followed the principle and international practice relating to the fixation of the BPT rate and recent trends regarding the level of rate of this tax. These countries levy BPT with a moderate flat rate as follows:

Table 3.6: BPT Rates in the EAC Countries

Country	Type of companies	Rate
Burundi	Normal rate	30%
Kenya	Resident companies	30%
	Non-resident companies	37.5%
Rwanda	Normal rate	30%
	Newly listed companies on capital market get rebate on tax rate based on the percentage of the sale of their shares to the public for a period of 5 years	Reduced rates

---

13   For the same reason, no basic allowances are granted to companies as they are to individuals.

14   One can argue, however, that since small companies have fewer resources than large companies, the former cannot compete with the latter. Consequently, some tax relief, e.g. a lower tax rate, may be granted to small companies.

15   George E. Lent, "Corporation Income Tax Structure in Developing Countries", IMF Staff Papers, 25(3), 1977, p.737.

16   For example, in the US, CIT rates were lowered from 48% to 46% in 1981 and to 34% in 1986. See also John Diamond, George Zodrow & Robert Carroll (March 2013). Macroeconomic Effects of Lower Corporate Income Tax Rates Recently Enacted Abroad, Ernst and Young LLP.

Country	Type of companies	Rate
Tanzania	Newly listed companies in the Stock Exchange with at least 30% of its share issued to the public	25%
	Other companies	30%
	Companies with perpetual tax loss for 3 consecutive years as a result of tax incentives on investment	0.3% of annual turnover
Uganda	Companies, other than mining companies, trustees, retirement funds	30%
	Mining companies rate is based on a formula, which can range between 25% and 45%	25-45%

Some EAC countries have different rates for types of companies in order to achieve various objectives. For example, Rwanda and Tanzania levy a lower rate BPT than the normal BPT rate on listed companies in order to encourage public companies and growth of the capital market.

The BPT and PIT rates are not aligned in some EAC countries, which invite economic inefficiency. For example, in Uganda as the BPT rate (30%) is lower than the top PIT rate (40%), the controlling shareholders are subject to an additional tax on distributed income, and this provides a tax advantage for companies that keep their savings in the form of retained profits, which inhibits dividend payments. Since these results are less than optimal from an economic point of view, it is desirable to align the BPT and PIT rates.

Some EAC countries have attempted to keep the BPT rate and the top marginal PIT rate at the same level in order to maintain neutrality in the choice between proprietorships and companies. For example, the top PIT and BPT rates are kept at 30% in Kenya, Rwanda, and Tanzania. Such an alignment of the BPT rate with the top marginal PIT rate is expected to prevent arrangements to avoid a higher tax rate by changing the legal status of an entity.

3.9. Taxation of permanent establishments

A foreign company may operate its business in a host country either through a branch/permanent establishment (PE) or a subsidiary. A subsidiary needs to be incorporated in the host country and is taxed like any other company incorporated in that country. The foreign company faces a limited liability of its subsidiary in the host country. On the other hand, PE is not incorporated in the host country. It belongs to the foreign company, which has to bear unlimited liability for debts and other obligations of its PE.

The term PE is commonly defined as a fixed place of business through which business of a foreign company is wholly or partly carried on. The International Tax Glossary defines a PE "as a place of management, a branch, an office, a factory, a workshop, a mine, a quarry or other place of extraction of natural resources, or a building site or assembly project which exists for more than a certain period (6 to 12 months) and in certain circumstances an agent or permanent representative." The use of facilities solely for purpose of storage, display or delivery of goods belonging to enterprise, purchasing offices, and agent's business premises are excluded from the definition of PE.

The concept of PE is adopted under both the OECD and UN model conventions. Under both model conventions, a PE is defined as a fixed place of business through which business of an enterprise is wholly or partly carried on. There are, however, some differences in the definition given under these two conventions. The definition of PE is broader under the UN model than under the OECD model convention. For example, under the OECD model convention a building site or construction or installation project constitutes a PE only if it lasts for more than 12 months, while the UN model convention reduces duration of the relevant site or project to six months.

The definition of PE is included also in the domestic tax laws of Rwanda, where a PE is defined as a fixed place of business through which the business of a foreign company is wholly or partially carried out. A PE may be an administrative branch, factory, workshop, mine, quarry or any other place for the exploitation of natural resources, and a building site or a place where construction or assembly works are carried out. However, a foreign company is considered as not to have a PE in Rwanda if that company:

- uses facilities solely for the purpose of storage or display of goods or merchandise;
- maintains a stock of goods or merchandise belonging to that person solely for the purpose storage or display;
- maintains a stock of goods or merchandise belonging to that person solely for the purpose of processing by another person;
- has a place of operation aimed purposely at purchasing goods or merchandise or of collecting information related to his or her business;
- has a place of operation solely for the purpose of carrying on preparations of his or her activities, and performing any other activities that make them more effective.

Similarly, a foreign company is not considered as a PE if it only carries out activities through a broker, general commission agent or any other private agent in accordance with procedures of the ordinary course of the activities of such an agent in Rwanda.

PE is generally used to determine whether a particular kind of income is or is not taxed in the country from which it originates. The existence of PE is a condition for the country where such establishment is located to be empowered to tax it. Profits derived from the activities of PE are taxed by the country where the income was obtained, i.e. the source country taxes income attributed to the PE while the income, which is not attributed to PE, is taxed by domicile country. Normally, a PE is treated as a separate entity and taxed only on income attributable to its own operations. For example, in Tanzania, a PE of a non-resident company is considered as a separate person from the non-resident foreign company.[17] The PE is taxed on its profit as well as repatriated income. Amounts derived/payments received and expenditure incurred/payments made for the purposes of assets held by, liabilities owed by or the business of the PE, are attributed to it for the purpose of Tanzanian taxation. The repatriated income is equal to dividends distributed by the foreign PE.

3.10. Tax payment

In the EAC countries, BPTs are levied on the basis of the self-assessment system, where a taxpayer is required to assess tax, submit returns and pay tax in a correct and timely manner. BPT is paid in three/four instalments in the EAC countries, which are calculated on the basis of the tax paid in the preceding year or on estimated income of the current tax period.[18] Instalments are prepayments. Adjustments are made at the time the final payment, when the difference between the prepayment and actual annual tax liability as calculated by the taxpayer himself. If the amount of the prepayment exceeds the actual annual tax liability, the excess is refunded to the taxpayer. The tax is to be paid at the bank or the tax office.

3.11. International taxation

As stated earlier, all EAC countries levy tax on the worldwide income of their resident taxpayers. This means they levy tax on the income earned

---

17   Tanzania, Government of. Section 70 of Income Tax Act 2004.
18   Instalment payments are generally reduced by the tax withheld in that tax period.

by their resident taxpayers within the country as well as abroad. The income earned abroad is also taxed by the country where it was earned. As a result, income earned by a resident taxpayer outside the country is taxed twice, once in the country where it was generated and once in the home country. For example, a Rwandan resident company, say ABC Company, carries out its business also in Uganda, which levies tax on the income generated by ABC Company in Uganda as a source country. The same income is also taxed by Rwanda as a country of residence of ABC Company resulting in international juridical double taxation.

3.11.1 Unilateral reliefs/bilateral agreements

Attempts have been made in the EAC region to avoid international juridical double taxation through unilateral relief, bilateral tax treaties or regional agreements. Under the unilateral relief method, measures are adopted to avoid international double taxation through domestic tax laws. EAC countries also follow this practice. Most EAC countries have completed some bilateral tax agreements[19] to avoid international double taxation. Besides, the EAC Council of Ministers approved the Community's double taxation treaty in 2010. While the agreement was expected to avoid double taxation and increase cross-border investments, it has not yet become operational.[20] Tax agreements further help combat fiscal evasion through the exchange of information. In general, provisions of the bilateral treaty override the provisions of the domestic laws relating to exemption, limited taxation or credit for foreign tax. Bilateral treaties are considered more effective than unilateral measures in avoiding international double taxation, which is necessary for the promotion of international economic activities.

3.11.2 Ordinary tax credit

EAC partner states have basically adopted a tax credit mechanism to avoid international double taxation under which resident taxpayers are allowed to claim a credit for the tax paid in the source country against their residence tax liability. Tax is levied on the total income of a resident, irrespective of its origin, and a credit is allowed for the tax paid in the source country.

---

19   Bilateral agreements are largely based on either the OECD model or the UN model or partly on the one and partly on the other. Some modifications are made at the time of completing the agreements to suit a particular situation.

20   See articles in The East African and in TradeMark East Africa: http://www.theeastafrican. co.ke/news/-/2558/2415362/-/5m0tn6z/-/index.html and http://www.trademarkea.com/ news/double-taxation-stumbling-block-towards-trade-boost-eac/.

EAC countries have adopted the ordinary credit system, where the maximum credit would be the tax to be levied at the rate of the residence country. In other words, credit will be allowed only to the extent that foreign tax rate that does not exceed domestic tax rate applicable to the taxpayer's taxable income. For example, in Uganda any foreign income tax paid by a taxpayer in respect of foreign-source income included in the gross income of the taxpayer in Uganda can be claimed as a credit, which should not exceed the Ugandan income tax payable on the taxpayer's foreign source income for that year.[21] Similarly, in Tanzania a resident taxpayer may claim a foreign tax credit for any foreign income tax paid on foreign income, which should not exceed the average rate of Tanzania income tax.[22] More or less similar provisions exist in Kenya[23] and Rwanda.[24] The implication is that, if the tax rates of foreign countries are higher than the domestic tax rates, there is a possibility that total foreign tax may not be offset completely.[25] On the other hand, if the rate of tax is lower in the source country than in the residence country, foreign tax credit is allowed for the income taxes actually paid to the source country.

3.11.3 Per country basis

In the EAC countries, foreign tax credit is granted on the per country basis[26] and such credit should not exceed the average rate of the domestic income tax applicable to the taxable foreign source income. Any unused credit is carried forward for unlimited period.

Foreign tax credit is calculated separately for each income year and any foreign income tax not adjusted due to the limitation in respect of any country may be carried forward, and is treated as paid with respect to assessable foreign income of the person for a future income year that is sourced in the same country.

In Uganda, the calculation of the foreign tax credit of a taxpayer for an income year is made separately for foreign-source business income and other income derived from foreign sources by the taxpayer during the year.

---

21   Uganda, Government of (1997). Section 81. Income Tax Act 1997.
22   Tanzania, Government of (2004). Section 77. *Income Tax Act 2004.*
23   Kenya, Government of (1974). Section 77. *Income Tax Act 1974.*
24   Rwanda, Government of (2005). Section 6. Laws on Direct Taxes on Income 2005.
25   On the other hand, under the full credit system, resident taxpayers are allowed to deduct from the domestic tax liability the total amount of tax paid in the other countries.
26   Foreign tax credit may also be granted on the overall basis. Under this system the amount of creditable taxes may be determined on an overall basis. An excess over the creditable limit can be carried forward for specified years.

3.11.4 Tax deductions

The Tanzanian Taxation Act also provides an option to the taxpayer to claim a deduction for foreign income tax for which a credit is available. Under the tax deduction system, foreign source income is added to the total taxable incomes of the resident, but foreign taxes are deductible to arrive at the net income. For example, if a Tanzanian company has paid BPT in Uganda in 2013, this amount can be deducted from the gross income of the company in order to determine the Tanzanian BPT liability.

Chapter 4

Value Added Tax

4.1. Introduction

All the EAC partner states levy VAT. This tax was initiated in the region by Kenya in 1990, followed by Uganda in 1996. VAT was introduced in mainland Tanzania in 1998 and in Zanzibar (which forms part of Tanzania) in 1999. Rwanda and Burundi adopted VAT in 2001 and 2009, respectively.

EAC VATs have been introduced by separate VAT laws. They have replaced various types of sales taxes and are administered by the respective revenue authorities in the EAC countries.

Table 4.1: Overview of VAT in the EAC

Description	Countries					
	Burundi	**Kenya**	**Rwanda**	**Tanzania**	**Uganda**	
VAT Law	Value Added Tax Act 2009	Value Added Tax Act 1989	Value Added Tax Code 2001	Value Added Tax Act 1997	Value Added Tax Act 1996	
VAT implemented on	1 July 2009	1 January 90	1 October 2001	1 July 1998 (1 January 1999 in Zanzibar)	1 July 1996	
VAT replaced	Transaction tax	Import-manufacturing level sales tax	Turnover tax	Sales tax, hotel levy and entertainment tax	Commercial transaction levy on services and sales tax on goods	
VAT threshold	BIF 100 million	KES 5 million	RWF 20 million	TZS 40 million	UGX 50 million	
VAT rates	18,10	16,12	18	18	18	

4.2. Evolution

4.2.1 Kenya

Kenya was the first EAC partner state to adopt VAT in the EAC and it implemented the tax in a phased manner. The VAT Act was passed on August 25, 1989 and implementation of VAT began from January 1, 1990 in a partial way. Initially, the new tax resembled in many ways its predecessor, sales tax.[1] For example, like sales tax, VAT was limited to the import-manufacturing point, it was levied with a standard rate of 17% along with 15 different higher rates, ranging from 20% to 210%,[2] it exempted many inputs[3] and was imposed only on a few specified services. The base of VAT was broadened in 1991 by making more services VATable. The VAT base was widened further in the following years and was fully implemented up to the retail level by 1996.The original VAT registration threshold was KES 300,000 for hotels and restaurants and KES 250,000 for others. The threshold was increased and unified over the years and has been fixed at KES 5 million per annum from January 1, 2007.The rate structure of VAT was rationalised in the 1990/91 budget, when the number of VAT rates higher than the standard rate was reduced from 15 to 6.[4] At the same time, the standard VAT rate was increased from 17% to 18%, and a 5% VAT was introduced on previously exempt items like most of the raw materials and capital goods.[5] The rate structure of VAT was further rationalised over the years. The tax is now levied with a standard rate of 16% and a reduced rate of 12% on the supply and imports of electricity and fuel.

4.2.2 Uganda

Uganda was the second country to adopt VAT in the EAC region. In the 1994 budget, the Finance Minister announced that VAT would be introduced from 1 July 1996. Preparation for the introduction of

---

1   Sales tax, which was introduced in 1973, was basically an import-manufacturing level sales tax. In 1989, the tax was levied with a standard rate of 17% together with a wide range of higher rates on luxury items. There was a provision for refund of tax paid on inputs in order to minimise the problem of double taxation and to refund tax levied on exports in order to promote exports. For details see Graham Glenday On Safari in Kenya: from Sales Tax to Value Added Tax. *International VAT Monitor*, December 1991, pp.2-3.

2   *International VAT Monitors*, January 1990, p.32 and September 1990, p.28.

3   Similarly, goods exempt under the Third Schedule to the Custom and Excise Act were deemed to be exempted under the VAT. See *International VAT Monitor*, September 1990, pp.28-29.

4   In 1990/91, VAT rates of 20%, 35%, 50%, 60%, 65%, 75%, 85%, 120% and 210% were eliminated.

5   *International VAT Monitor*, September 1990, p.28.

VAT began in July 1994.[6] To this end, a steering committee was formed and a VAT Implementation Unit was created in the Uganda Revenue Authority (URA). Similarly, a VAT Consultative Committee, consisting of both government and private sector, was also set up.[7] URA officials were trained on VAT.[8] Some URA officials also visited Ghana, Kenya and South Africa to learn about the workings of VAT.[9] They educated the public about VAT through seminars, publications and the media.

A draft VAT law was prepared and circulated for public comment, and was passed by the parliament on December 27, 1995. It received presidential assent on March 23, 1996 and the tax was introduced from July 1, 1996[10] when the VAT replaced the sales tax/commercial transaction levy.[11] VAT was initiated with a standard rate of 17% and the level of threshold was fixed at UGX 20 million. VAT was intended to broaden the tax base, raise more revenue and remove cascading.

Despite the introduction of VAT after two years of detailed preparation, VAT implementation did not go without a hitch in Uganda, owing particularly to a large number of registrants (about 14,000) caused by a low registration threshold and poor screening.[12] VAT was opposed by smaller traders,[13] who went on strike in September-October 1996. In response to this, the registration threshold was increased from UGX 20 million to UGX 50 million in November 1996 and a large number of taxpayers were deregistered. Another change introduced in July 1997 was the transfer of several items from the zero rated list to the exemption list to ease VAT administration.

While the standard VAT rate was increased from 17% to 18% from July 1, 2005, it was reduced from 18% to 5% on the sale of residential property from July 1, 2007. However, the sale of residential property was exempt from VAT from July 1, 2009.

---

6   Justin O.S. Zake, The Introduction of VAT in Uganda: Avoiding the Great Ghanaian Debacle. *International VAT Monitor*, 7, 2, 1990, p.60.
7   *Ibid*, p.60.
8   *International VAT Monitor*, (1995). 6, 2, p.131.
9   *International VAT Monitor*, (1995). 6, 2, p.132.
10   *International VAT Monitor* (September/October 1996), p.303.
11   Sales tax, introduced in 1969, was levied at the import-manufacturing point on a wide range of imported and domestically produced goods with multiple rates. (See *International VAT Monitor* (October 1990), p.30.) The Commercial Transaction Levy was levied on commercial services, including accommodation, advertising, clearing and forwarding, legal practice, printing, consultancy, banking, restaurants, construction, and motor vehicle repairs.
12   IMF (1998). IMF Country Report, 98,61, June,1998, pp.5-6.
13   Not the larger trading and manufacturing community who understood the benefits of a VAT.

4.2.3 Tanzania

Tanzania stood third in the row of VAT implementing countries in the EAC region. In 1991, the Mtei Commission on tax reform recommended the introduction of VAT in place of sales tax.[14] In the 1996/97 budget session, government announced its intention to introduce VAT.[15] The VAT Act was enacted in 1997, originally scheduled to be implemented from January 1, 1998 but was postponed for further preparation. VAT registration began on January 1, 1998 in mainland Tanzania, where the tax went live on July 1, 1998[16] with a standard rate of 20% and a threshold of TZS 20 million. As Zanzibar was even less prepared, VAT implementation in Zanzibar was delayed further, where VAT was adopted on January 1, 1999 with a standard rate of 20% and a lower threshold of TZS 15 million. In the wake of problems encountered by Ghana and Uganda in the introduction of VAT, Tanzania moved more cautiously in the implementation of VAT.

The registration threshold was increased from TZS 20 million to TZS 40 million on July 1, 2004.[17] The VAT rate was reduced from 20% to 18% from July 1, 2009.[18]

4.2.4 Rwanda

In Rwanda, introduction of VAT was taken as the first phase in a general reform of tax intended to streamline public finance.[19] To prepare for the introduction of VAT, a VAT Implementation Project was set up. It commenced work in December 1998 with a committee subdivided into sub-committees with different responsibilities geared towards the introduction of VAT. Tax officials were trained on VAT and taxpayers were educated about the new tax before its introduction.

On 27 April 2000, the Transitional National Assembly adopted a law introducing VAT.[20] It was introduced in 2001 in place of a turnover tax (ICHA). Original threshold was RWF 15 million per annum (or RWF 3.7 million last calendar quarter). This was, in December 2004,

---

14   Sales tax, introduced in 1969, was basically an import-manufacturing level sales tax. It was levied with multiple rates on a wide range of commodities, including inputs and final products resulting in cascading. The tax was collected at importation on duty paid value and at the point of sale by manufacturers, at the time the goods were removed from its premises. See *International VAT Monitor* (September 1990), p.33.

15   *International VAT Monitor* (June 1999), p.118.

16   VAT replaced sales tax, stamp duty, hotel levy and entertainment tax, applicable to VAT registered businesses.

17   Tanzania, Government of (2005). Budget Speech 2004/05, p.68.

18   Tanzania, Government of (2010). Budget Speech 2009/10, p.61.

19   *International VAT Monitor* (December 1999). 10, 6, p.287.

20   *International VAT Monitor* (2000), p.170.

increased to RWF 20 million per annum (or RWF 5 million in the preceding calendar quarter) or is likely to exceed either of these figures in the coming years. The original standard rate of VAT was 15% which was increased to 18% in 2003.

4.2.5 Burundi

In Burundi, the Finance Minister granted approval for necessary preparations for the introduction of VAT in April 2006.[21] VAT was introduced in place of the transaction tax[22] from July 1, 2009. This was aimed at achieving multiple objectives such as to boost business, attract foreign investors, help regulate informal trade, increase the efficiency of tax collection, harmonise the tax system with other EAC countries and offset potential losses in customs revenue due to accession to the EAC. The standard rate of VAT was fixed at 18% and the registration threshold was determined at BIF 100 million.

4.3. Existing structure

4.3.1 Nature

All EAC countries have adopted a standard destination based,[23] consumption type,[24] tax credit method[25] VAT. These countries levy

---

21   IMF (2006). IMF Country Report. 06/311, p.45.
22   The transactions tax, which was introduced in 1968, was levied on varieties of goods and services at 7%, 17% and 20%, depending upon the nature of goods. For example, 7% was levied on agricultural products, 17% on imports, and manufactured goods, and 20% on sales of cigarettes, wine and luxury vehicles.
23   While the tax is levied on exports but not on imports under the origin based tax, the tax is levied on the commodities that are destined for consumption in the country irrespective of their origin and exports are relieved from the burden of VAT under the destination based tax.
24   There are three types of VAT. They are: consumption type, income type and gross national product type. These types vary in the treatment of capital goods. Under the consumption type VAT, all capital goods purchased from other firms are excluded from the tax base in the year of purchase while depreciation is not deducted from the tax base in the subsequent years. Since investment is relieved from taxation under this type, the base of tax is consumption. The income type VAT does not exclude capital goods purchased from other firms from the tax base in the year of purchase. This type, however, does exclude depreciation from the tax base in the subsequent years. The tax falls both on consumption and net investment. The conceptual tax base of this type is the net national income. On the other hand, under the gross national product type VAT, neither capital goods purchased by a firm from other firms are deductible from the tax base in the year of purchases nor depreciation is deductible from the tax base in the subsequent years. Hence tax is levied both on consumption and gross investment. The conceptual tax base of this type is gross domestic product.
25   VAT can be calculated by means of tax credit, addition or subtraction method. Under the tax credit method, tax is levied on the total value of sales and taxpayers are permitted to deduct from their gross tax liability the taxes already paid by their suppliers and passed on to them. On the other hand, under the addition method, the tax base is obtained by

VAT on all commodities destined for domestic consumption, but relieve exports from the burden of VAT. In all the EAC countries, VAT paid or payable by VAT registrants on all kinds of goods, including capital goods and services to be used in the supply of taxable goods and services, is deductible from the tax collected or collectable by them on their supplies and the difference is remitted to the government as net VAT. For example, if the taxable purchases of a vendor are USD 100 and taxable sales are USD 150, the vendor is required to pay a VAT of USD 10 on his purchases and to collect USD 15 on his sales, at the rate of 10% VAT. The tax paid on purchases is known as "input tax," while the tax collected on sales is known as "output tax." The vendor can deduct his input tax from output tax and remit the balance to the treasury. In the above example, VAT payable to the treasury is USD 5 (USD 15 - USD 10 = USD 5).

There are some exceptions regarding the allowable input tax credit in the EAC countries. For example, input tax credit is denied on business entertainment and passenger cars in countries like Kenya, Tanzania and Uganda. In Burundi, input tax credit can be taken only up to 50% of input tax paid on investments. Denial of input tax credit in this manner works against the essence of VAT, where VAT ceases to be tax on value added and becomes just turnover tax.

4.3.2 Coverage

EAC VATs cover all goods and services except those exempt[26] by law. In other words, VAT laws of these countries specify goods and services that are exempt from tax and those not included in the exemption list are subject to VAT. There has, however, been a wide practice to grant exemptions under the VAT system in the EAC countries. For example, the Kenyan VAT Act "grants exemption to 395 goods and 22 categories

---

adding the incomes produced by the firm. In other words, the tax base is computed by adding the payments made by the firm to the factors of production employed in turning out the product, such as wages, interest, rent, and profits. Under the subtraction method, value added is determined as net turnover, which is obtained by subtracting the cost of materials from sales proceeds.

26   Exemptions under the VAT means exemption of outputs/sales while the items still carry a tax element levied on inputs. It must be remembered that as tax-exempt goods and services are kept outside VAT net, their suppliers can neither collect VAT on their sales nor can claim refund of the tax paid on purchases or imports. This means that while there is no tax on the outputs, there is a tax on their inputs, which cannot be claimed as an input tax credit but can be passed on to the consumers in the form of higher prices.

of services."[27] In these countries, exemptions have been provided to achieve different objectives as follows:[28]

- Some items are exempt from VAT for social reasons. For example, basic food items are exempt from VAT for reasons of equity. Necessary items such as these attract a larger portion of income of the lower income groups than that of the higher income groups. Hence there is a presumption that exemption of necessities helps to achieve some degree of progression by relieving a large part of income of the poorer section from the tax net. Similarly, educational and health services, wheel chairs, and public passenger transport services are exempt from VAT on social grounds. One, however, does not know how far these exemptions are effective in achieving distribution objectives as the rich may purchase proportionately large amounts of goods and services that are exempt on distribution ground, thereby benefiting more than the poor by exemption policy.

- Some exemptions are provided on economic grounds. For example, Kenya and Tanzania exempt tourist services to promote tourism. Agricultural tractors and machinery, fertilizers, insecticides, and herbicides are commonly exempt from VAT for the promotion of agriculture. Further, industrial machinery is exempt in Rwanda and Uganda for industrial development. However, as in the case of exemption provided to achieve a social objective, one does not know how far exemptions granted to achieve economic objectives are effective in achieving the same. This is because under the VAT system, those who fall inside the tax net can take input tax credit and those who remain outside the tax net have to pay the tax on purchases, but cannot deduct the input tax amount from output tax or claim for a refund of an excess credit, though they can recoup the paid VAT by increasing the price of their supplies.

---

27   Patrick Mtange, ICPAK Position Paper on the VAT Bill 2012, Institute of Certified Public Accountants of Kenya, p.1.

28   For details see Schedules II (exempt goods) and III (exempt services) of VAT Act 1989 of Kenya, Schedule II of VAT Act 1996 of Uganda, Schedule II (Special Relief in Schedule III) of VAT Act 1997 of Tanzania, and Article 86 of the VAT Act of Rwanda.

- Some items are exempted from VAT on administrative grounds. For example, EAC countries largely exempt financial[29] and insurance[30] services from VAT as it is difficult to determine value added in the case of these services.[31]

- Other common exemptions may include exemptions of postage, stamp, coins, land and buildings. Similarly, imports or purchases by various levels of government, central banks, diplomatic missions/personnel or donor funded projects, are also commonly exempt from VAT.

4.3.3 Threshold

EAC countries collect VAT at all stages in the process of production and distribution. This means that importers, manufacturers, wholesalers and retailers are required to register for the purpose of VAT. However, businesses with a taxable turnover below the registration threshold are not required to register for VAT irrespective of their position in the production and distribution chain. The VAT registration threshold is fixed to keep petty vendors out of the VAT net as they may find it very difficult to comply with VAT formalities and may have to bear high compliance costs.[32]

In all the EAC countries, the VAT registration threshold is fixed on the basis of turnover.[33] For the purpose of the calculation of the registration threshold,[34] the value of all taxable supplies, including the

---

29   Financial services are exempt from VAT on administrative grounds. VAT cannot be levied on gross interest charged by financial institutions since the whole interest amount is not value added of these institutions. Value added is only a fraction of spread rate (difference between borrowing and lending rates), which constitutes, in addition to the service charge other such items such as risk of the loan and rate of inflation. It is also not easy to identify service charges in the case of the provision of any loan, advance or credit, the issue and sale of shares etc. In other financial services such as foreign exchange, moneychangers may include their commissions in spread rate (difference between buying and selling rates) instead of charging a commission separately for the exchange of currency. As it is difficult to levy VAT on core financial services, they are exempt from VAT. VAT, however, can be levied on some financial services where the consideration for services can be specifically identified. For example, bank charges for the rental of the safe deposit box, fees for bank advice, and subscription fees for credit cards, in which cases it is easy to find the service charge.

30   Like financial services, it is not simple to levy VAT on life insurance services, as the premium may contain a saving element in addition to service charge. That is why EAC countries have exempted these services from VAT.

31   It is also difficult to determine the value added in gambling, lottery, etc.

32   The VAT system becomes difficult to administer if very small, unorganized vendors are brought under the tax net. There is a high possibility that the net revenue may be eaten away by costs of collection. This explains why a threshold is required under the VAT system.

33   While some countries take into account number of employees, or capital investment, to determine turnover, in some other countries, if a person has more than one business, he is required to register, irrespective of his level of transactions.

34   Value of taxable goods and services is calculated before adding VAT.

supply of zero-rated items, is taken into account. It is to be noted that the supply has to be made in the course of furtherance of taxable businesses in order to include it in the calculation of threshold. However, sales of a capital asset, such as machinery used in the manufacturing process of the business, is not included in the calculation of threshold although a registered business is required to charge VAT on such sales. Similarly, value of tax exempt goods and services and out of scope supplies[35] is not included in the calculation of the registration threshold.

Countries like Kenya, Tanzania and Uganda have adopted both the retrospective and prospective basis of calculating the threshold. While these countries determine registration threshold on the basis of the value of sales of the taxable transaction in the last twelve months or a quarter, they also consider registration threshold on the basis of the estimated turnover in the following twelve months or quarter. For example, in Uganda, a business is required to register for VAT if its annual turnover in the last 12 months was above UGX 50 million or above UGX 12.5 million in the last quarter. Similarly, if a business expects its annual turnover to exceed UGX 50 million in the following 12 months or exceed UGX 12.5 million in the following quarter, it is required to register.

Table 4.2: Level of Threshold in the EAC Countries

Country	Annual Threshold	
	National Currency	US Dollar (May 2014)
Burundi	BIF 100 million	65,147
Kenya	KES 5 million	57,937
Rwanda	RWF 20 million	29,629
Tanzania	TZS 40 million	24,125
Uganda	UGX 50 million	19,747
Simple Average		39,317

The level of threshold varies significantly among the EAC countries. The average threshold in these countries is USD 39,317. While Burundi and Kenya have a higher than average threshold, others have lower. It is the highest in Burundi while the lowest is in Uganda. EAC countries

---

35   For example, in Singapore, transfer of business or part of a business is considered out of the scope supply.

have adopted one threshold for all types of taxpayers,[36] which is administratively easy to handle. The EAC's average threshold is similar to New Zealand's threshold, much higher than the common threshold adopted by EU countries which is in the neighbourhood of USD 13,000, but much lower than the UK's threshold which is fixed at USD 106,600. The EAC's average threshold is lower than Ghana's threshold (USD 60,000) and higher than Nepal's threshold (USD 21,300).

4.3.4 Rate

EAC countries have adopted a simple rate structure. Rwanda, Tanzania and Uganda have adopted a single positive rate of 18%, while Kenya has adopted a standard rate of 16% and a lower rate of 12% on the supply and import of electricity and fuels. While Burundi also levied VAT with a single rate of 18% until 2012, it has introduced a lower rate of 10% for agricultural products, livestock and imported food.

Table 4.3: VAT Rates in the EAC Countries

Country	VAT Rates % (2013)	
	Lower	Standard
Burundi	10	18
Kenya	12	16
Rwanda		18
Tanzania		18
Uganda		18
Simple Average		17.6

The standard simple average rate of VAT in the EAC region is 17.6%. Burundi, Rwanda, Tanzania and Uganda have higher and Kenya has lower rates than the EAC standard average rate. In general, EAC VAT rates are in the range of VAT rates of many countries, lower than the rates of European countries, particularly Scandinavian countries where VATs are levied at 25%, and higher than the VAT rates of some developing countries such as Nigeria (5%), Papua New Guinea (10%) and Nepal (13%). The EAC countries' VAT rate structure is more or

---

36   There is an issue of having one or different thresholds for different lines of business or stages in the production and distribution process. Some argue that manufacturers should be required to register irrespective of their level of transactions. On the other hand, others argue that the size of turnover is important, not the place of business in the production or distribution stage. Still others argue that there should be separate thresholds: one for goods and another for services.

less harmonised. A uniform rate is the beauty of the VAT system in the EAC region since such a rate is easy to administer as there is no need to classify goods and services into different groups and taxpayers are not required to keep separate records, which reduces both administrative and compliance costs and maintains administrative efficiency. Similarly, a single rate avoids producers or consumers diverting their resources to lower rated commodities to save on tax. It maintains economic neutrality.

4.3.5 Zero-rating

EAC countries zero-rate exports to relieve them from the burden of VAT. As zero-rated goods and services are treated at par with other taxable goods and services, tax paid on the inputs of exports can be claimed as input tax credit/refund by the exporters. On the other hand, as exports are subject to VAT at the rate of zero percent, they actually do not attract any tax. As both inputs and outputs are relieved from the burden of VAT, exports do not carry any element of VAT in the international market. Thus VAT does not hamper the competitive power of the domestic products of the EAC countries in the international market.

There is also a common practice in the EAC countries to zero-rate food and other items supplied to any transport leaving the country for consumption or sale in the transport itself outside the country. Some EAC countries such as Rwanda also zero-rate supplies made to diplomats and diplomatic missions, donor funded projects and other privileged persons and organisations. Besides, several other items are zero-rated in most of the EAC countries. For example, Uganda has zero-rated medicines, educational materials, milk, seeds, fertilizers, pesticides and hoes and domestically produced cereals; Tanzania has zero-rated domestically produced agricultural inputs, domestically supplied human and veterinary drugs, and mosquito coils, and supply of locally manufactured sacks and fishing nets, while Rwanda has zero-rated supply by a tour operator or travel agent, licensed as such, to a tourist of an inclusive tour. On the other hand, Kenya has granted zero-rate status to a total of 416 supplies, both goods and services,[37] including milk, medicaments, vitamins, seeds, fertilizers and agricultural machinery.

---

37   Patrick Mtange, *op. cit.*, p.1.

4.4. Operation

4.4.1 Registration/de-registration

In the EAC countries, suppliers of taxable goods and services are liable to register either when their total taxable turnover of the past 12 months or any other specified period exceeds the registration threshold or the taxable turnover in the coming 12 months or any other specified period is likely to cross the threshold.[38] The person liable to register for VAT must register by submitting an application for registration in the prescribed form within 20 days in Uganda and 30 days in Kenya from the date on which she/he becomes so liable. Suppliers of taxable goods and services having total annual turnover below the registration threshold can apply for voluntary registration in most EAC countries, including Kenya, Rwanda and Uganda.

There is also a provision for forced registration in some EAC countries. For example, in Kenya, Tanzania and Uganda, if tax authorities are satisfied that a business is required to register, they can issue an order to the taxpayer asking him to register. On the other hand, the tax authority can refuse registration in some countries such as Uganda when the tax commissioner has reasonable ground to believe that the person is not fit for registration.

In Kenya, a registration certificate must be issued within 10 days after the receipt of application for registration by the tax office and the effective date of registration is the date mentioned in the certificate as date of registration. In Kenya and Uganda change of information included in the application for registration needs to be provided to the tax office within 14 days. The corresponding period is 30 days in Tanzania. The tax registration certificate must be displayed in the main place of business and a certified copy in other places of business.

In the EAC countries, a VAT registrant can apply for de-registration when he closes his transactions or when his transactions go below the registration threshold. For example, in Kenya, when the taxable supply goes below KES 5 million in 12 months, the taxpayer should notify the tax

---

38   However, specified vendors are required to register irrespective of the level of turnover in some countries. For example, in Kenya dealers of motor vehicle spare parts, electronics, timber, jewellery and professional services are required to be registered irrespective of turnover. In Uganda designated professionals were required to register for VAT irrespective of their level of threshold from 2002 to 2008. In Tanzania, the Commissioner of TRA may register any person regardless of his taxable turnover for the protection of revenue or on grounds of national economic interest.

commissioner of the value of his supplies and apply for deregistration.[39] In Uganda, tax administration can cancel the registration of a taxpayer who fails to file a tax return or is considered not fit for registration on other grounds. Such a business remains liable for payment of any taxes due, even after the cancellation of VAT registration.

4.4.2 Invoicing and accounting

As stated earlier, EAC countries have adopted the tax credit method of VAT calculation, which is also known as the "invoice method." This is an invoice driven system, where the tax invoice is the most important document. A VAT registered seller is required to issue a serially numbered tax invoice in respect of each sale to another VAT registered vendor, while a VAT registered buyer is also required to take and preserve invoices in order to claim an input tax credit/refund. In case of sales by a VAT registrant to non-registrants, a receipt should be issued.

Tax invoices are issued in duplicate in Uganda and Rwanda, the original is given to the buyer, who needs to preserve it for the purpose of claiming input tax credit and the copy is retained by the supplier in his records. In Uganda, when the original tax invoice is lost, the buyer may request the seller to issue a copy of tax invoice, which should be marked prominently "copy only."

In some countries, retailers can issue a simplified tax invoice for sales to unregistered customers and for low value transactions. For example, in Uganda, a simplified tax invoice can be issued by a vendor, whose annual taxable turnover is below UGX 100 million, to another registered vendor when the value of an individual item does not exceed UGX 50, 000 and the total invoice does not exceed UGX 100, 000. In Kenya, a simplified invoice can be issued in respect of cash sales from retail outlets.

In EAC countries such as Kenya, Rwanda and Uganda, taxpayers can issue debit/credit notes under certain situations, where it will be necessary to make adjustment in the amount of tax stated in the tax invoice. For example, in Uganda, credit notes can be issued by a VAT registered supplier to the VAT registered recipient when tax is over charged on invoice and debit notes when tax is under charged on the invoice. It is common to issue debit/credit notes in two copies, original to be given to the recipient and duplicate to be maintained in the suppliers' record.

---

39   The business then will be subject to turnover tax under income tax.

VAT registrants are required to maintain purchase and sales books to list each sale and purchase. They are also required to prepare a VAT account in some countries such as Kenya and Rwanda, which is a monthly statement of total purchases, sales, input tax, output tax and payable/refundable VAT.

In the EAC region, VAT is based on the accrual accounting method, where taxpayers are required to account for VAT on the basis of tax invoices issued and received. However, small taxpayers are allowed to maintain cash basis accounting in some countries. For example, in Uganda, vendors with an annual taxable transaction below UGX 200 million may select cash basis accounting, which needs to be adopted in case of both output tax and input tax and must be maintained for at least two years after its adoption. In Tanzania, retailers are required to use electronic cash registers to record their daily sales and issue receipts for all transactions.

There are different practices in the EAC countries regarding the period for the maintenance of accounts. For example, accounts must be preserved for 5 years in Burundi and Kenya and 6 years in Uganda.

4.4.3 Tax period, return submission and payment of tax

While the standard tax period is one month in the EAC countries, there are some exceptions relating to small vendors. For example, in Rwanda, the tax period is quarterly for businesses whose annual turnover is equal or less than RWF 200 million, although taxpayers voluntarily can submit returns on a monthly basis.

A VAT registrant is required to file a tax return in prescribed form for a tax period to the tax office concerned within 15 days after the end of tax period in Rwanda and Uganda, 20 days in Kenya,[40] and 30 days in Tanzania. In Uganda and Rwanda, taxpayers are required to submit two copies of the return in prescribed form. The original is kept by the tax office and the duplicate is returned to the taxpayer with the tax office stamp as a proof of submission of return.

In the EAC countries, while the VAT on imports needs to be paid at the time of importation in case of domestic supplies, it must be paid to the government account on a tax period basis within 15 days after the end of the tax period in Rwanda and Uganda, 20 days in Kenya and 30 days in Tanzania.

---

40   In Kenya, Form VAT 3 is the VAT return. Form VAT 3A should be attached with the
      credit return. Form VAT 3B needs to be completed and attached with the return in case of
      zero rated supplies.

Kenya introduced a system of withholding VAT on October 1, 2003. Under this system, governmental organisations, banks, financial institutions, insurance companies, cooperative societies and regular exporters were appointed as VAT withholding agents, who were required to deduct VAT at source on the payment of VATable goods and services purchased from VAT registered or non-registered vendors, and directly deposit the deducted amount to the treasury. They were also required to issue a VAT withholding certificate to the suppliers indicating the VAT withheld, which was equivalent to the tax invoice for purposes of taking an input tax credit or claiming a refund. Rwanda also applies withholding to government bodies on payments made to VAT registered persons.[41]

Withholding systems provides an incentive even to the small businesses – whose transaction is below the registration threshold but sell to the withholding agents – to register under the VAT in order to apply for refunds which they pay to the withholding agents. Besides, some businesses which remain in a more or less permanent net credit position often request for refund. This has added complications in the VAT administration.[42]

4.4.4 VAT refund

In the EAC countries, in general, excess input tax is immediately refunded to the exporters. For example, in Uganda, excess credit may be refunded within one month of the due date for the return or within one month from the date when the return was made if the return was not made by the due date. However, when the amount of excess tax is less than UGX 5 million, except in the case of an investment trader or person providing mainly zero-rated supply, excess credit may be offset against the future liability of the taxpayer. Besides, even when excess credit is above UGX 5 million, with the consent of a taxpayer, the excess credit may be offset against the future liability of the taxpayer or may be adjusted with any other tax liability of the taxpayer. Government has to pay interest at a rate of 5% point higher than the prevailing official bank rate of Bank of Uganda for the delayed period. Such a system is desirable from both the taxpayers' and collectors' point of view as taxpayers can offset excess credit with the future liability and do not have to apply for

---

41   PWC. *Doing Business: Know Your Taxes*, East African Tax Guide 2012/13, PWC, March 2013, p.47.
42   Nada O. Eissa & William Jack, Tax Reform in Kenya: Policy and Administrative Issues. Initiative for Policy Dialogue Working Paper Series, Georgetown University, October 2009, pp.14-15.

refund and the tax collectors do not have to process a large number of refund claims. It was found that a large number of taxpayers choose not to claim refunds, but use large excess input tax credits declared on one return to offset subsequent VAT liabilities over a much extended period.[43]

In Kenya, a VAT registrant can apply for refund in case of zero-rated supplies as well as tax withheld by appointed VAT withholding agents[44] within 12 months from the date of tax becoming payable.[45]Application for refund of tax of KES 1,000,000 or more should be supported by a certificate issued by an independent auditor.[46]

In case of non-exporters, excess input tax credit is treated differently in different countries. For example, in Uganda, excess input tax credit is first adjusted with any tax due amount and the remaining amount is either refunded[47] or carried forward to the next tax period, depending upon the choice of taxpayers. In Kenya, an excess credit is carried forward to the next tax period. Excess credit is carried forward up to 6 months, if not adjusted, then refunded in Tanzania, where all refund claims are to be examined by a registered auditor who issues a "certificate of genuineness." In this country, there is a provision to pay interest to the refund claimant when properly submitted refund claims are not paid within 30 days.

In Rwanda, a taxpayer can apply for refund of an excess input tax credit by submitting a VAT return in the normal way. To establish a claim for refund, the return must show excess input tax credit for the current tax period as well as any excess input tax credit amount carried forward from a preceding tax period. Upon receipt of the claim, the tax administration determines whether or not verification would be necessary prior to the payment of refund. If verification is not required, refund should be made within 30 days of the end of the prescribed period for filing return or the date of receipt of the return, whichever is

---

43   Eric Hutton, Mick Thackray, & Philippe Wingender Revenue Administration Gap Analysis Program – The Value-Added Tax Gap, April 2014, p.27. See www.finance.go.ug/index.php?option=com_docman&Itemid.

44   In Kenya when a non-registered person exports, he may claim a VAT refund for tax paid on import or paid to a registered supplier by submitting Form VAT 4.

45   A longer period up to 24 months is possible if allowed by the Commissioner.

46   Nada O. Eissa & William Jack *Tax Reform in Kenya: Policy and Administrative Issues*, Initiative for Policy Dialogue Working Paper Series, Georgetown University, October 2009, p.26.

47   Within one month after the receipt of return or claim for refund in the case of taxpayer with a monthly tax period, and within two months after the receipt of return or refund claim in the case of taxpayers with quarterly tax period.

later. If verification is needed, the deadline to refund approved claims[48] is extended to three months and the taxpayer needs to be informed about it. If the claimant owes any tax, then the tax administration may set-off the approved refund amount against the due tax. Failure to issue refund within this date attracts an interest of 1.5%.

4.5 Summary

All EAC members levy VAT. EAC VATs have been largely harmonised in terms of their basic design as they follow the destination principle, adopt consumption type and tax credit methods, cover all the goods and services except those specifically exempt by the law, and apply a uniform rate at the same level. They, however, vary considerably in terms exemptions, zero-rating and workings. This indicates the need to harmonise these aspects by limiting exemptions to a few items and zero-rate to exports, in order to make VAT aligned to its basic principle so that the tax can be more efficient from both economic and administrative points of view, revenue productive, and responsive to economic changes. It is also necessary to harmonise the operational aspects of VAT so that, among others things, it becomes easy to follow by the business community across the region.

Those East African Countries such as South Sudan that are considering including VAT in their tax systems should learn from the experience of existing VAT levying countries. They should adopt the good aspects of the existing EAC VATs such as adoption of the destination principle, consumption type and tax credit method, application of a uniform rate, fixation of one level of registration threshold for all types of businesses and zero-rating to exports. They should, however, be wary of the bad aspects of other EAC VATs such as the plethora of exemptions, excessive application of zero-rating, VAT withholding and zero-threshold in case of specified dealers. It is to be kept in mind that a detailed preparation for the introduction of VAT in terms legislation, operating manuals, guidelines, institutional set-up, training of tax officials and education of taxpayers is a must in order to implement VAT in a proper and effective manner. International experience indicates that, in general, countries have taken 18 to 24 months to prepare for introduction of VAT. East African Countries may take even longer as their tax administrations are weak, there is a lack of billing practice in the market, and accounting systems have not been developed amongst the business community.

---

48   If a refund claim is rejected, the taxpayer will be informed with the reasons for rejection.

Chapter 5

Excise Duties

5.1 Introduction

While in the past excise duties were levied mainly on domestic products destined for home consumption,[1] modern practice is to levy these duties on domestic production or on import of excisable goods and on provision of excisable services. As in sales tax/VAT, excise duties are levied on commodities (goods and services) and are classified as indirect taxes. However, unlike sales tax/VAT which are general in nature, excise duties are selective. This means while sales tax/VAT are levied on all goods and services except on items exempt by the law, excise duties are levied, as stated by Adam Smith, "only upon a few sorts of goods"[2] that are categorised as excisable goods and excisable services by the law. Hence the common practice around the world is to specify excisable items under excise laws. This approach is also followed by EU Council Directive concerning the general arrangements for excise duties.[3]

EAC partner states have adopted a modern excise duties regime, where taxes are levied on the domestic production or import of excisable

---

1   Adam Smith (1776). *The Wealth of Nations*, Introduction by Robert Reicb, The Modern Library, New York, 2000, p.947.

2   *Ibid*, p.947.

3   EU (2008). EU Council Directive 2008/118/EC of 16 December.

goods and provision of excisable services. While excise duties in the EAC region are broadly guided by the East African Excise Management Act (EACMA), member countries have adopted national excise laws to operate excise duties in the respective countries. For example, excise duties are levied under the Customs and Excise Act in Kenya, the Excise Law No. 26/2006 in Rwanda,[4] the Excise (Management and Tariff) Act in Tanzania, the Excise Tariff Act in Uganda and Decree Law No. 01/02 in Burundi. As elsewhere, excise duties are based on the destination principle in the EAC region, meaning that they are levied on goods destined for domestic consumption irrespective of their origin. This also means that both domestically produced and imported goods are treated uniformly and the duties are not discriminatory. On the other hand, exports are spared from the burden of excise duties. EAC countries collect excise duties basically at the import/manufacturing point as it is relatively easier to collect tax at an early stage in the process of production and distribution due to the limited points of tax collection and the relatively more organised nature of taxpayers, basically manufactures.

5.2 Types of excise duties and their objectives

As any other taxes, excise duties are levied to generate revenue in the EAC region. These duties on average provide around 19% of total tax revenue and 17% of total revenue of EAC countries, where the excise tax revenue to GDP ratio is about 3%.[5] In addition to generating revenue, excise duties also contribute to achieving socio-economic objectives in the EAC countries. For example, these countries invariably levy "sumptuary excise duties" with a view to reduce the consumption of goods that lead to socially undesirable effects. Tobacco products and alcoholic beverages are considered to be harmful to the health of consumers. Traditionally excise duties on these items have been justified on health grounds. In this context, Adam Smith wrote: "It has, for some time past, been the policy of Great Britain to discourage the consumption of spirituous liquors, on account of their supposed dependency to ruin the health and to corrupt the morals of the common people."[6] Besides, the consumption of alcoholic beverages generates costs in the form of "increased automobile accidents, drinking related crime and

---

4   Rwanda, Government of (2006). Excise Law No. 26/2006 of 27/05/2006 Determining and Establishing Consumption Tax on Some Imported and Locally Manufactured Products in Rwanda.
5   Simple average of figures in Tables 1.6, 1.7 and 1.8 in Section 1.5.
6   Adam Smith, *op. cit.*, p.962.

maintenance of alcohol abuse centers."[7] Similarly, the consumption of tobacco products increases the health care burden on society. Tobacco and alcohol use imposes costs even on individuals who do not consume them. The recent trend is to take into account such negative externalities also. Other attractions to levy excise duties on tobacco products and alcoholic beverages are their large sale volumes, the price-inelastic demand,[8] and lack of close substitutes.[9] This makes sumptuary excise duties productive and efficient. Besides, it is politically easy to levy "sin taxes" or to raise their rates as the consumers of alcoholic beverages and tobacco products cause high social costs, i.e. costs on society and on themselves.[10]

EAC countries also levy "luxuries excise duties" on such items as motor cars, cosmetics, perfumes and soft drinks. These duties are levied to check the demand for luxury items and divert resources to the desired sectors. Luxury excise duties also complement VAT, which is commonly levied at a flat rate in order to maintain efficiency, both economic and administrative. This tax is supplemented by excise duties on luxury items to inject progressivity into the tax system. Furthermore, excise duties on soft drinks are levied also due to other reasons such as their high visibility and are usually produced by foreign companies with good compliance habits. Moreover, they are easy to tax, their administration is manageable, they are alleged to cause health problems and it is not likely to cause major political uproar over the imposition of tax on these items.[11]

Excise duties are also levied in the EAC region in the form of "benefit excise duties" on such items as gasoline and vehicles. These duties are based on the benefit principle of taxation and are charged as user charges to generate revenue for construction of roads and their maintenance. These excise duties are further justified as the use of fuels and vehicles may also cause negative externalities through air, water and

---

7   Roy Bahl, Taxing Soft Drinks, International Studies Program Working Paper 11-06, Andrew Young School of Policy Studies, Georgia State University, April 2011, p.8.

8   "The addictive nature of nicotine implies low price elasticity of demand and, among smokers, a large sales volume." Sijbren Cnossen How Should Tobacco Be Taxed In EU-Accession Countries? CESIFO Working Paper No. 539, August 2001, p.11.

9   Sijbren Cnossen, Excise Taxation in Australia. Chapter 10 in *Australia's Future Tax and Transfer Policy Conference*, Melbourne Institute, 2010, p.236.

10   For example, as stated above, heavy drinking not only brings harmful effects on the health of the consumer but also leads to violent behaviour and causes accidents. See Sijbren Cnossen, "Alcohol Taxation and Regulation in the European Union," CESIFO Working Paper No. 1821, Category 1: Public Finance, October 2006, Presented at CESIFO Conference in Public Sector Economics, April 2006, p.2.

11   Roy Bahl, *op cit.*, p.2 and p.22.

noise pollution and causing congestion. For example, "Individual road users impose various costs on other road users, and on society as a whole, through the effects of their travel and transport decisions, on pollution, traffic congestion, accidents, and the physical deterioration in the road infrastructure."[12] Besides, excise duties on petroleum products are also used to conserve energy and reduce the dependence on imported oil.

5.3 Commodity coverage and classification

EAC countries levy excise duties basically on traditional excise carriers such as tobacco products and alcoholic beverages, and a few other items. All members of the EAC levy excise duties on tobacco products and alcoholic beverages. Similarly, gasoline is subject to excise duties in all these countries, which also levy excise duties on vehicles. Besides, it is common to levy excise duties on carbonated soft drinks, mineral water, juice, and telecommunication services in the EAC region. Plastic bags[13] are taxed in Uganda, Tanzania, and Kenya, while powdered milk is taxed in Rwanda and cement in Uganda. Kenya has expanded the coverage of excise duties by including many cosmetics and perfume items[14] in the excise net.

Some EAC member countries such as Tanzania and Kenya have adopted the Harmonised System of commodity classification to define excisable items by reference to a Harmonised System based code number[15] due to its several advantages, including facilitation of tax administration by making it easier to apply excise rates uniformly across importers/manufacturers. It also helps in avoiding linguistic differences

---

12   Stephen Smith, Taxes on Road Transport in Southern African Countries, Revised version of a paper presented at the South African Conference on Excise Taxation, Pretoria, South Africa, 11-13 June 2003, p.1.

13   Non-biodegradable plastic bags are banned in Rwanda.

14   These items are: manicure or pedicure and other makeup preparations, shampoos, hair lacquers and other preparations for the use of hair, lip and eye make-up preparations, pre-shave, shaving and after-shave preparation, perfumes, personal deodorants and antiperspirants, perfumed bath salts and other bath preparations, depilatories and other perfumed, and cosmetic or toilette preparations. Since there are no other goods which are similar to these items and subject to excise duties, there is no possibility of resources being diverted away from the production/consumption of taxed goods to untaxed goods and violating the principle of fiscal efficiency.

15   The Harmonised System, which was developed by the World Trade Organization in connection with customs duties, classifies goods into 21 Chapters, 96 Sections and 5018 Headings. It has been adopted widely worldwide, including in the EAC region, where it is mandatory for the member countries to adopt the system under the Protocol on the Establishment of the East African Customs Union to harmonise the tariff nomenclature at the 8-digit level.

and potential disputes regarding definition of excisable goods,[16] and makes it possible to generate comparable statistics across the countries.

5.4 Rate of excise duties

EAC countries levy excise duties with specific or *ad valorem* rates. While specific rates are fixed on physical units of excisable items such as weight, length, size, packet etc., *ad valorem* rates are expressed in terms of price. Examples of specific rates are: excise rate on beer per litre USD 2, cigarettes per 1,000 sticks USD 30, cement per metric ton USD 100, textiles per metre USD 3 and sugar per kg USD 1; examples of *ad valorem* rate are: excise rate is 25% of customs value on motor cars or 10% of ex-factory price on soft drinks.

Of the East African countries, Burundi, Rwanda and Tanzania levy excise duties on an *ad valorem* basis on some items and on a specific basis on others. Kenya levies *ad valorem* rates on some items, specific rates on others. It also fixes rates on both a specific and an *ad valorem* basis on some other items, whichever is the higher rate being the effective rate. For example, in case of wine, the excise rate is KES 70 per litre or 35% of the value, whichever is higher and on liquor, KES 120 per litre or 35% of the value, whichever is higher. There is also a practice elsewhere to levy excise duties with an element of both specific and *ad valorem* rates. Under such a system, the excise rate on wine, for example, could be fixed as per litre USD 5 plus 20% of price.

The reasons behind the fixation of rates on both specific and *ad valorem* basis might be to make the excise system responsive to price changes by means of *ad valorem* rates and at the same time to safe-guard revenue from decreases due to under-statement of the excisable value (i.e. ex-factory price or customs value) through specific rates. Such a system, however, complicates tax administration.

Sumptuary excise duties are commonly levied with specific rates as they are considered more effective to discourage the consumption of health hazards and to reduce negative externalities.[17] Specific rates are

---

16   Ben J.M. Terra, Chapter 8 Excises, Victor Thuronyi, (edit.), *Tax Law Design and Drafting,* Vol. 1, International Monetary Fund, Washington, DC, p.7.

17   Sijbren Cnossen, Excise Taxation in Australia. Chapter 10 in Australia's Future Tax and Transfer Policy Conference, Melbourne Institute, p.241; Emil M. Sunley, Ayda Yurekli & Frank J. Chaloupka, The Design, Administration, and Potential Revenue of Tobacco Excises, Chapter 17, in Prabhat Jha & Frank Chaloupka (edits), *Tobacco Control in Developing Countries, Oxford University Press 2000,* p.411, and AM Center for Public Policy Studies and International Tax Investment Center, A Special Report on Addressing Harmonization of Excise Regimes in the East African Community: Petroleum, Alcohol, Tobacco, Soft Drinks and Mobile Communication, Spring 2007, p.9.

considered easier to administer as they require minimum paper work and investigation, and do not invite the problem of valuation. Specific rates establish a clear link with external costs and make the tax definitive and transparent since the taxpayers know exactly what they will have to pay in the form of tax. This also facilitates revenue forecasts[18] or enhances the predictability of excise revenue. Besides, since specific rates put higher burden as a percentage of their value on low quality goods, producers are encouraged to improve the quality of their products under the specific tax regime.

Specific rates, however, are considered regressive and inelastic and need to be increased frequently in response to inflation to keep the value of tax revenue unchanged in real, inflation-adjusted terms. Frequent changes in the rates may not be easy from a political point of view, particularly during the time of high inflation, as the increase in the tax rate "will just make inflation worse"[19] and may cause administrative problems, as both taxpayers and tax collectors have to learn about them almost every year if these rates are adjusted annually in line with inflation.

On the other hand, *ad valorem* rates make the excise system elastic/buoyant[20] as they provide for an automatic increase in revenue with the increase in price.[21] As taxes that are responsive to price changes increase revenue automatically, they are considered equitable. In this respect, *ad valorem* rates are desirable to levy on luxury items such as motor vehicles and telecommunication services.

Ad valorem rates, however, as discussed later, encourage taxpayers to understate the value of their products to lower the tax

---

18   Emil M. Sunley et al., *op. cit.*, p.411.

19   Benn Terra, *op. cit.*, p.4.

20   Tax revenue increases because of increase in National Income. But it is also influenced by discretionary changes (i.e. changes in rates, bases, imposition of new taxes and improvement in tax administration). The automatic growth (i.e. increase in tax revenue only because of increase in National Income) is measured by income elasticity while discretionary changes and automatic changes together (i.e. total change in tax revenue due to all conceivable factors) are measured by buoyancy.

21   However, not everyone agrees with this view. It may be that when excise duties are levied on the ex-factory price, there is a tendency among the manufacturers to suppress the ex-factory price to pay less excise duties even though there might be a substantial increase in prices beyond the tax point. A Power Point Presentation on "Excise on Tobacco Products" was presented by British-American Tobacco, Eastern Europe, Middle East and Africa at a Regional Public Private Dialogue on Harmonization of Domestic Taxes in the EAC organised by East African Business Council and the East African Community Secretariat in collaboration with the TradeMark East Africa, Africa Capacity Building Foundation and the International Financial Corporation as part of the Network of Reformers in Dar Es Salaam from 11th -12th November 2011.

liability. In response to this, some countries try to levy excise tax on retail price while others try to artificially fix excisable price which complicates tax administration and is not in line with market principle. Further, *ad valorem* rates may induce producers to compromise quality, aiming at producing cheaper goods to lower excise liability.

Other features of the excise tariff in the EAC region are as follows:

- Some EAC countries have adopted local content rule where goods made out of local materials are either exempt or taxed lightly compared to goods made out of imported materials. For example, in Tanzania wine made with the domestic grape content exceeding 75% are subject to zero percent vis-à-vis TZS 1,053 per litre on other wines. Similarly, in Uganda, beer from at least 75% local materials excluding water is subject to 20% excise tax while the corresponding rate is 60% on beer made out of imported materials.

- Some EAC countries have adopted graduated rates in case of some items in order to inject progressivity in the tax system. For example, in Kenya, excise duties are levied with graduated rates on cigarettes depending upon type (such as plain, soft cap and hinge lid) and price of cigarettes.

- Excise rates on gasoline vary considerably depending upon nature such as premium and regular gasoline, diesel and kerosene.

- Some countries such as Tanzania levy higher rates on vehicles with higher engine capacity than ones with lower engine capacity.

- Excise duties on alcoholic beverages are levied on the basis of the alcohol strength; high alcohol content means more damaging effects on health, so higher rates to discourage its consumption.

5.5 Operation of excise duties

In the EAC countries in general, the base of excise duties in the case of imports is the customs value and in the case of domestic products, the ex-factory price, which includes the cost of production and the profit of the manufacturer. In the case of services it is the selling price.

As excise duties are generally levied at high rates, they encourage importers or manufacturers to understate the value of excisable items. In response to this, tax officials are authorised to adjust the excisable value. In the case of imports, customs valuation procedures apply also to determine excisable value, where, in the absence of transaction value, customs value is determined on the basis of World Trade Organisation (WTO) prescribed valuation methods.[22] In the case of domestic

---

22 In the absence of price actually paid or payable for the imported goods, customs officials can determine value on the WTO prescribed methods which are: transaction value of

products, tax officials are given power to adjust excisable value on the basis of the fair market value to address the problem of valuation.[23] Appropriate valuation and assessment procedures are important not only from the revenue point of view, but also to maintain fairness among taxpayers and hence to make the tax system equitable.

Now, let us turn to the calculation of excise duties with the help of an example. Let us suppose XYZ Company produced 100 bottles of wine of 1 litre each and the ex-factory price of one bottle is USD 15. Let us examine the scenarios with different types of excise duties rates:

(i)   When the excise rate is USD 5 per litre:

Items	Quantity	Excise rate	Excise liability
Wine	100 bottles	USD 5 per litre	USD 500

(ii) When the excise rate is 20% of the ex-factory price

Items	Quantity	Unit price	Total price	Excise rate	Excise liability
Wine	100 bottles	USD 15	USD 1,500	20%	USD 300

(iii) When the excise rate is USD 5 per litre or 20% of ex-factory price, whichever is higher being the effective rate:

As calculated above, the excise tax revenue is USD 500 at the rate of USD 5/per litre and USD 300 at the rate of 20% of ex-factory price. As the revenue is higher under the specific rate, it will be the effective rate and excise liability will be USD 500.

(iv) When the excise rate is USD5 per litre and 20% of ex-factory price:

As calculated above, the excise amount is USD 500 with the specific rate and USD 300 on the basis of the ad valorem rate, so total excise liability under such a rate structure would be USD 800 (USD 500 plus USD 300).

---

identical goods, transaction value of similar goods, deductive method, computed method or the fall back method.

23   It is to be noted that *ad valorem* excise rate encourage manufacturers to set up an artificial sales depot at the factory gate or to appoint persons related to them as dealers, sell to the sales depot or dealers at a lower price, pay less tax, increase the sales depot's or dealer's price and reap a large amount of profit. Excise laws of some countries have defined excisable value as the selling price or fair market value, whichever is higher. This means, if excise officials are not satisfied with the price declared by the manufacturer, they can determine excisable value on the basis of the dealer's commission, transportation cost, consumers price in the nearest market and so on.

Excise duties on imports are collected from the importers of excisable products at customs points at the time of importation along with customs duties. While excise duties liability is created in the case of domestic products at the time goods are released outside the production/distribution premises and in the case of excisable services, at the time when excisable services are provided, producers of excisable goods and providers of excisable services are required to assess their tax liability, pay tax and submit excise returns on a tax period basis within a specified time. For example, in Rwanda, for the purpose of the payment of excise duties a month is divided into three periods as follows:

- From 1 to 10 of every month,

- From 11 to 20 of every month, and

- From 21 to the end of every month.

Here, an excise payer is required to submit an excise return together with the proof of payment of excise duties to the tax office within five days following each tax period. While such a frequent system of payment of excise duties maintains a continuous flow of resources into the treasury and the tax collected by the manufacturers is paid promptly to the government, it creates a lot of inconvenience to the manufacturer as a manufacturer has to submit 36 returns in a year which increases his compliance costs. Thus the system is expensive for the taxpayers. This also increases the cost of collection as tax officials have to deal with the taxpayers more frequently. So it could be replaced by a monthly filing and payment system, so that the manufacturers would have to submit only 12 returns in a year as against the current number of 36 returns. This would not only reduce the expenses of the manufacturers, but also reduce the workload of the tax administration.

5.6 Excise control

As elsewhere, excise duties have been subject to various types of controls in the EAC countries. For example, the EACMA and Excise Acts of various EAC member countries require a manufacturer to obtain a license and renew it annually in order to produce, manufacture, process and hold excisable goods.[24] It is necessary to obtain a separate license

---

24   This is also true in many other countries, including Australia: "The Australian excise licensing system would be considered quite rigid in the context of many other excise-type licensing or registration systems, and places considerable onus on the applicant to demonstrate that they are a bona-fide business with the full set of resources and skills for dealing in excisable goods. Further, that both the business and key personnel have sound

for each factory in which excisable goods are manufactured and for each class of excisable goods[25] to be manufactured.

A licensee, before the commencement of the production, must indicate each building, room, and place within the factory premises to be used in the manufacture, preparation for sale or storage of materials or excisable goods. He/she is also required to maintain equipment such as scales, weights, lights, ladders etc. in the factory. A manufacturer should notify the excise administration of any modification to the premises or any changes to the functioning of the factory and increase, repairs or replacement of one or more equipment or tools.[26] A manufacturer is also required to provide suitable accommodation to the excise officer posted at the factory to maintain control of excisable goods.

Traditionally, excise duties were run purely under the physical control system in different countries. Under this system, an excise officer was posted at the factory. A manufacturer who obtained license for the manufacture of excisable goods had to obtain permission from the excise officer concerned for the commencement of manufacture. As production began, the manufacturer had to send samples of his products to the excise administration to have them certified by the excise officer, and, in the event of any change in such goods, samples of such goods had to be sent as well. A manufacturer had to store his products in a warehouse situated within the premises of the factory, to be locked in duplicate by himself and excise personnel posted at the factory. He had to maintain a register as specified by the excise rules containing account of his daily production, the quantity deposited in the store room, and the quantity taken out of his factory. The manufacturer had to fill in

compliance records in all taxation matters, and that there are no other aspects that put the excise revenue being generated by the business at risk of not being paid or being paid late." See Rob Preece "Key Controls in the Administration of Excise Duties", *World Customs Journal*, 2, 1, 2008, p.79.

25   Items of similar nature are included in one class of excisable goods. For example, cigarettes, cigars and manufacture tobacco are treated as one class of excisable goods. This is also true in many countries around the world, as Preece states "a single excise activity such as distillation of spirits, refining of crude oil, supply of lottery tickets, recycling of motor vehicles tires etc. and to be conducted at a single business address or location, such as street address" (Preece, *op. cit.*, p.79).

26   "The result of scoping licenses in this manner is to restrict the applicant to a single activity, or single range of related activities, at known and identifiable locations. The objectives of such restrictions are to allow administering agencies to control the nature of operations that will be conducted and to be able to reconcile such risk factors as the nature of the business applying for a license against the type of operation for which the license is sought" (Preece, *op. cit.*, p.79).

a demand form in order to clear the excisable goods from the excise warehouse which had to be countersigned by the excise officer posted at the factory. It was also necessary to pay excise duties before removing the excisable goods from the factory warehouse. Such a system existed in several countries, including Nepal, Scotland and the United Kingdom. In Scotland, once whisky distilleries "had official locks on their entrances, exit door to the distillery, and no activity could take place without the officer being present to unlock the locks." A similar system existed in the United Kingdom, where "each bonded warehouse used to have a resident officer who had to unlock and lock the warehouse."(27)

As the system of posting excise officers at the factories was expensive for the government, corruption-prone and costly as well as inconvenient to the factory owners, over the years it was replaced by the "self-removal procedure" and a record based control system. Under this system, a manufacturer is permitted to assess excises himself and remove goods from the factory without the approval of an excise officer, but his documents and accounts are checked by excise officers periodically to ensure that the amount due to government has been properly assessed and paid. This has been the common practice globally these days,(28) including the EAC member countries where a manufacturer is required to maintain records relating to the manufacture, storage and delivery of excisable goods and materials, which must be made available for inspection by an excise officer any time. An excise payer must keep a register of raw materials,(29) an activity register(30) and a register of inventory(31) of manufactured goods. An excise payer is also required to keep a sales register which should indicate the price and quantity sold to every customer with customer's name and address. A visiting excise officer must sign in such a register during every visit to the factory.

Excise duties are levied when goods are removed for consumption from the factory/tax warehouses. They are not levied on the transfer of

---

27   Emil M. Sunley, et al., *op. cit.*, p.417.
28   For example, "the United Kingdom relies on the warehouse keeper to exercise day-to-day control with official control based on spot checks and system of audit. Some developing countries might need to consider similarly intensive controls on tobacco products. As in all such systems, however, the potential for fraud by the excise officer would have to be considered." (Sunley, E.M., *op. cit.*, p.417).
29   Description of the materials to be used in manufacture of taxable products.
30   Description of the information concerning the daily status of every equipment used in the factory.
31   Description of the products destroyed, discarded or burnt after being inspected by the authorised officer, the quantity exported and those sold for consumption so that at any time the quantities within the factory can be established and verified.

goods between authorised warehouse keepers and on exports.[32] In these cases, goods are transported under the duty suspension arrangement when goods may be released under a transfer bond or export bond, and must be accompanied by documents issued by the consigner. The EACMA has provisions relating to security where a producer of excisable items may be required to give security in the form of a bond or cash deposit, or partly bond and partly cash deposit, for due compliance and protection of the excise revenue.[33]

In some countries, excise duties on tobacco products and alcoholic beverages are controlled through the use of stamps/banderols/levels/ stickers affixed to cigarette packages and stamps affixed to the crown or cork of liquor bottles.[34] For example, in Rwanda, manufactures and importers are required to affix a tax stamp on the specified excisable products. Stamps are supplied by the tax office. A licensee is required to submit to the authority a monthly reconciliation statement of stamp showing the following within 10 days of the end of the month covered by the statement:

- Stamps in stock brought forward from the previous month,
- Stamps received from the Authority,
- Stamps applied to taxable products,
- Stamps spoiled or damaged as certified by the Authority staff,
- Stamps unaccounted for in the reconciliation statement, and
- Stamps in stock at the end of the month and carried forward for use in the following month.

The process followed in Kenya regarding excise stamps on cigarettes and alcohol is as follows:

- Excise stamps are supplied by the Kenya Revenue Authority (KRA) to the manufacturers and importers of cigarettes and liquors;
- They are serially numbered and bear an ultraviolet working court of arms and the words *KRA*; and
- They should be affixed on tearing joint of all bottles/containers of alcohol/ cigarettes in such manner that shall be clearly visible and damaged on opening the bottle or container.

---

32   Similarly, supplies made to diplomatic missions, foreign aided projects, and airplane/ ship's stores are not subject to excise duties. Excise duties are also not levied on losses and destruction of stock.

33   The East African Excise Management Act, Section 36.

34   As sometimes fake stamps/stickers may be used to avoid tax, they require strong security system. For pros and cons see http://www.taxstampforum.com/about-the-forum/14-3rd-forum/general/62-review-of-3rd-tax-stamp-forum

Excise stamps are used not only as pre-payment, full or partial, but also as anti-avoidance and anti-counterfeiting of excisable products.[35]

5.7 Excise duties under a common market

Excise duties need to be harmonised under the common market for its proper functioning. Harmonisation may take place in terms of the items subject to excise duties, product definition, tax base, tax rates, and procedures regarding the imposition and collection of excise duties.

Attempts have been made to harmonise excise duties under various economic unions, including the EU, where member states agreed in 1972 to adopt a common excise framework.[36] An EU council directive was introduced in 1992[37] in relation to the excisable commodities and their holding, movement and monitoring. The directive was replaced by the Council Directive 2008/118/EC that provides direction regarding the levy of excise duties by the member states. It specifies objects of excise duties,[38] basis for fixing tax rates, time and place of chargeability of excise duties, excise control mechanism, exemptions and so on.

As excise duties are levied on domestic consumption, only excisable goods produced within or imported into the EU are subject to excise duties while goods exported outside the EU are relieved from the burden of excise duties.[39] Regarding excise rates, discussions were initiated to harmonise them across the EU. As it has not materialised, the concept of determining minimum rates and target rates has emerged. Finally it was agreed to fix only minimum rates of excise duties on certain items such as alcoholic beverages and tobacco products. There has also been consensus to levy specific rates on these items. Overall progress regarding the harmonisation of excise duties in the EU has, however, been minimal.

Discussions have been initiated to harmonise excise duties in the EAC region also in order to avoid market distortions and to promote

---

35   Rob Preece, *op. cit.*, p.85.
36   AM Center for Public Policy Studies and International Tax Investment Center, *op. cit.*, p.11.
37   Council Directive 92/12/EEC of 25 February 1992 on the general arrangements for products subject to excise duty and on the holding, movement and monitoring of such products.
38   The directive specifies alcohol and alcoholic beverages, manufactured tobacco and energy products and electricity as excisable items and specifies least minimum rates of excise duties to be levied on some excisable items such as wine, beer and cigarettes.
39   For the same reason, goods taken by travellers outside the community and sales to diplomats, international organisations, goods supplied on board aircraft or ship during the flight or sea crossing to outside EU territory or goods sold by tax-free shops are not subject to excise duties.

economic integration. Article 83(2) of the Treaty for the establishment of the EAC provides that partner states shall "harmonize their tax policies with a view to removing tax distortions in order to bring about a more efficient allocation of resources within the Community." A customs union was set up in 2005 and a common market in 2010. A few steps taken for the eventual harmonisation of excise duties between member states of the EAC have been as follows:

- EAC countries have adopted the EACMA;[40]

- The Permanent Secretaries of Kenya, Tanzania and Uganda Finance Ministries agreed, during the fiscal affairs committee meeting of the EAC held in 2005, to start the excise harmonisation process by setting minimum rates on petroleum products, alcoholic beverages, cigarettes and soft drinks;[41]

- A Special Report was prepared on "Addressing Harmonization of Excise Regimes in the EAC: Petroleum, Alcohol, Tobacco, Soft Drinks and Mobile Communication" by the AM Center for Public Policy Studies and International Tax and Investment Center in Spring 2007;

- A technical work group, representing tax policy and administration unit staff of the member states, was established in 2010 to study the excise systems of member states, identify divergences and their potential implications, and recommend measures for their harmonisation;

- The East African Business Council organised a regional workshop on June 29 and 30, 2010 in Arusha, Tanzania on the harmonisation of excise duties in the EAC region;

- An "East African Community Taxation Workshop" was organised by the Uganda Revenue Authority (URA) in Kampala, Uganda from April 26 to 28, 2011 in order to discuss coordination of indirect taxes, including excise duties in the EAC region; and

- A "Regional Public Private Dialogue: Harmonization of Domestic Taxes in the East African Community" was organised by the East African Business Council and the EAC Secretariat, in collaboration with the TradeMark East Africa and the International Financial Corporation as part of the Network of Reformers, Dar es Salam, Tanzania on 11-12 November 2011.

There is, however, a long way to go to harmonise excise duties in the EAC region. There are vast differences in the excise systems of member states in terms of excise policy, law, excise procedures, excisable items, tax base, tax rates, and filing and payment requirements. There are also

---

40   Consolidated East African Excise Management Act Chapter 28 of 1970 and Amendments up to Excise Management (Amendment) Bill 2003.

41   AM Center for Public Policy Studies and International Tax Investment Center, *op. cit.*, p.2.

vast differences in the economic situation of the member countries. Member states may not want to lose tax sovereignty. Harmonisation is not easy if the EU experience is any indication.

However, as large differences in excise rates induce smuggling and cross-border shopping, particularly in case of light items such as cigarettes that are easy to conceal and transport, member countries may continue reducing the large differences in the excise system among the member countries, increasing cooperation and information sharing between the tax authorities and adopting the best practices to minimise evasion and enhance revenue.[42]

5.8 Summary

EAC member countries levy excise duties on tobacco products, alcoholic beverages, gasoline, vehicles, soft drinks and a few other items. Excise duties provide, on an average, 15.5% of total tax revenue and 2.7 % of GDP in the region. There are wide differences among the excise systems, including the basis of levying excise rates and their level, which cause distortion, smuggling, and cross border legal shopping. This indicates the need for harmonisation of excise duties between the member states. Harmonisation can take place in terms of excise policy, law, taxable products, product definition, basis for fixing tax rates and their level, tax base, tax calculation, payment and filing procedures, which is of course not easy due to different circumstances in the sovereign member states.

There are some commonly agreed and implemented aspects of modern excise duties in the EAC countries. These include:

- limited to tobacco products, alcoholic beverages, gasoline, vehicles, and a few other luxury goods and services;
- levied with specific rates on tobacco products, alcoholic beverage and gasoline as these rates establish a clear link with external costs and do not require product valuation (particularly important at the import stage); thus, they contribute greatly to certainty in taxation;
- imposed with *ad valorem* rates on luxury items that make the excise system elastic and equitable;
- subject to some kind of control such as use of tax stamps or bar codes in order to secure government revenue;

---

42   *Ibid.*, p.2.

- operated under the self-assessment system with monthly filing and payment requirements; and

- not levied on the intra-community movement of excisable items to registered recipients.

Chapter 6

Customs Duties

6.1 Introduction

Customs duties are levied in the form of import and export duties. While import duties are levied on goods arriving in the country, export duties are imposed on goods departing from the country. Import duties are levied on a large number of items, while export duties are levied on limited specified products. Customs duties are basically levied on value with ad valorem rates (i.e., levied as percent of customs value). They can also be levied with specific rates (levied on the basis of some kind of physical units of goods such as kilogram, litre, packet or metre).

Historically, import duties have been used to achieve multiple objectives. They have been levied from time immemorial[1] to generate government revenue. It was easy to collect revenue from imports since the international trade sector was monetised relatively earlier than many other sectors; these duties are collected at a few points, such as ports, airports and border passes; and these duties are less complicated than other taxes such as income taxes, property taxes or VAT. In addition, the import sector grew substantially over the years. As a result, import sector has emerged as an important source of government revenue and customs duties provided a significant portion of total tax revenue

---

1   Adam Smith, *op. cit.*, p.947.

in the EAC countries. However, as a result of trade liberalisation and implementation of customs union in the EAC, these duties have become less important in the recent years as they provide less than 10% of total tax revenue of the EAC Partner States.

Import duties are also used as protective duties to guard domestic infant industry for a certain period of time, till it reaches a certain size and can face international competition. Apart from revenue and protective purposes, import duties are also used to improve balance of payment situation through restricting the consumption of imported goods.

Export duties are used to raise government revenue, to protect local processors of primary commodities, to prevent exports of some domestic products needed at home, to encourage domestic use of exportable products, to discourage rapid depletion of domestic resources and to stabilise the domestic economy, isolating it from the impact of the fluctuations of the world market.

It is, however, to be noted that customs duties are considered economically inefficient due to the following reasons:

- As customs duties are levied on commodities at an early stage in the process of distribution, (i.e. tax point is far from the final consumers) they cause a pyramiding effect due to the application of mark-up to customs duties inclusive prices by the vendors in the process of distribution.

- Customs duties increase the cost of doing business as unloading and unpacking goods, and packing and loading them again is expensive.

- Customs duties make domestic products less competitive in the international market due to the increase in cost of production of domestic products as a result of the application of customs duties on inputs of exports. While, as discussed later on, attempts are made to relieve exports from import duties through such schemes as duty draw back or bonded warehouse, these schemes are prone to misuse, collusion and corruption and are costly to administer.

- Customs duties become even more inefficient, both economically and administratively, if they are designed poorly and if customs procedures are made unnecessarily complex. For example, if customs duties are levied with too many different rates, they open scope for misclassification of goods (i.e., traders may be tempted to classify higher rated commodities as lower rated ones), legal disputes, collusion and corruption, and provide an opportunity to the lobbyists to put pressure on politicians/policy makers for the application of lower rates on their products. All these might lead to a decline in government revenue. A plethora of exemptions also lead to similar consequences.

- Besides, the structure of the customs duties cannot be determined independently, in isolation of the customs policies of the neighbouring countries. This is because differences in the rates of the customs duties of the neighbouring countries encourage smuggling and underground activities.

- That is why there is a trend around the world to rely less and less on customs duties as revenue and protective measures. In this context, both the level and number of customs rates have been stepped down in the recent years in various countries. This has simplified customs duties and reduced the scope for collusion and corruption. Customs duty reforms have further been directed towards the adoption of a uniform rate at low level due to the following reasons:

- A low level uniform rate is administratively simple as it avoids the problem of wrong classification of goods and potential legal dispute.

- Such a rate avoids the valuation problem as importers are not induced to classify their goods wrongly to lower their tax liability.

- It avoids scope for collusion and corruption regarding classification and valuation and the resultant revenue leakage.

- As the customs administration does not have to be involved in classification and valuation problems under the uniform customs rate, they can concentrate on other important activities including control of smuggling.

- Under the uniform rate, policy makers do not have to face undue pressure from lobbyists for the application of lower rates on their goods.

- A uniform rate facilitates border tax adjustment as it is easier to provide the exact amount of duty drawback/refund for the tax levied on the inputs of exports.

- Uniform rate also avoids the possibility of a situation where higher duties are levied on raw materials or intermediate goods than on the final products.

- A low level uniform rate is also economically efficient as it does not induce traders to change their economic decision in response to custom duties.

In order to avoid the cost of customs duties and facilitate trade[2], customs duties have even been dismantled completely on the goods crossing political boundaries of the member states of economic

---

2   Customs-duties-like internal duties levied on the goods crossing some kind of administrative boundaries of a country have been abandoned by almost all countries because of their ruinous effects on internal trade and commerce, since they require long hold up of transport, resulting in great delay and waste.

unions such as EU[3], ASEAN[4] and North American Free Trade Area (NAFTA)[5]. Some efforts have been made in this direction in the South Asian Association for Regional Cooperation (SAARC)[6] and the Free Trade Areas of Americas (FTAA)[7]. Several economic unions that have been created in Africa[8] also have been moving towards this direction. Some countries have also lowered the customs tariffs during the process of becoming members of the WTO.

6.2 Customs administration developments in the EAC region

EAC countries created a Customs Union effective January 1, 2005. The Protocol establishing the EAC Customs Union was signed by Kenya, Tanzania and Uganda on March 2, 2004, and was implemented from January 1, 2005. Burundi and Rwanda joined the union in 2008 with the application of protocol from July 2009. The Customs Union intends to:

- further liberalise intra-regional trade in goods on the basis of mutually beneficial trade arrangements among Partner States,

- promote efficiency in production within the Community,

- enhance domestic, cross-border and foreign investment in the Community, and

- promote economic development and diversification in industrialisation in the Community.

EAC member states agreed to:

- eliminate internal tariffs progressively within a transitional period of 5 years.

- adopt a common external tariff with 0%, 10% and 25%.

- remove all non-tariff barriers, and ensure that no new non-tariff barriers be imposed.

---

3   EU members are: Austria, Belgium, Bulgaria, Cyprus, Czech Republic, Denmark, Estonia, Finland, France, Germany, Greece, Hungary, Ireland, Italy, Latvia, Lithuania, Luxembourg, Malta, Netherlands, Poland, Portugal, Romania, Slovakia, Slovenia, Spain, Sweden and the United Kingdom.

4   There are ten members of ASEAN, which are: Brunei, Cambodia, Indonesia, Laos, Malaysia, Myanmar, Philippines, Singapore, Thailand and Vietnam.

5   Canada, Mexico and the USA are members of NAFTA.

6   Afghanistan, Bangladesh, Bhutan, India, Maldives, Nepal, Pakistan and Sri Lanka are members of SAARC.

7   It covers about four dozen countries of South America and the Caribbean.

8   Such as the African Economic Community, Common Market for Eastern and Southern Africa, Community of Sahel-Saharan States, East African Community Customs Union, Economic Community of Central African States, Economic Community of Western African States, South African Customs Union, and Southern African Development Community.

- exchange standardised and harmonised customs and trade information.
- adopt the "Harmonized System."
- facilitate and liberalise trade.
- adopt other measures including: rules of origin, national treatment, anti-dumping measures, subsidies, countervailing measures and safeguards which are briefly mentioned below:

Rules of origin: Rules of origin are the criteria used to determine the nationality of a product:

Preferential rules of origin are used to determine whether certain products originate in a preferential receiving country or trading area and hence qualify for trade preference.

Non-preferential rules of origin are used for all other purposes, including enforcement of product and country specific trade restrictions that increase the cost of entry (anti-dumping duties) or quotas.

National treatment: Goods produced within the EAC region are treated in an equal footing in all the EAC countries irrespective of their origin.

Anti-dumping measures: EAC member states have agreed to adopt anti-dumping measures when goods from any outside EAC country are sold in the EAC market at less than the normal value (i.e., less than the price at which the goods are sold in the home market). East African Community Customs Management Act 2004 (EACCMA 2004) has given authority to the member states to collect an anti-dumping duty.

Subsidies: A member state must notify other member states when it intends to grant any form of subsidy that might directly or indirectly distort competition. EACCMA 2004 allows the member states to levy a countervailing duty on goods upon which subsidies has been given in the home country of such goods.

Countervailing duty: Member states may levy countervailing duties on the importation of goods into the EAC region in order to offset the effects of subsidies provided in the home country of such goods.

Safeguard: Member states may take safeguard measures in order to mitigate the negative impact on domestic products due to the sudden surge of imports from outside EAC region.

Common customs law: Member states have adopted a common customs law, which is EACCMA 2004.

6.3 Existing structure

6.3.1 Scope

EAC countries do not levy customs duties on the movement of goods between the member countries. They have dismantled internal tariffs under the protocol of the establishment of the EAC Customs Union, which prevents a member state to levy such duties on the import of goods produced in other member states. Within the EAC region, there is a duty free movement of goods that are produced in the EAC member countries.

EAC countries, however, do levy import duties on goods crossing the boundary of the EAC region. In other words, they levy import duties on the import of goods from other countries to the EAC member countries or impose export duties on goods leaving the EAC region for other countries. Duties levied on the goods entering into the EAC region from outside are known as "common external tariff", which are levied on the import of a wide range of goods, except goods that are specifically exempt.

Several items have been exempt from customs duties in the EAC region. EAC Member states have agreed to harmonise their exemption regime. To this end, a harmonised list of exempted goods has been adopted under EACCMA 2004.[9] The list is rather long, which has several administrative, revenue, and economic implications. For example, exemptions complicate customs administration as there is a need to distinguish between taxed and tax exempt items, which is often not easy. They narrow the tax coverage and cause decline in revenue, which might necessitate levying import duties at higher rates on taxed commodities. As higher rates give incentive for tax evasion/smuggling, they further complicate tax administration, in addition to generating higher cost to the economy. This indicates the need to progressively reduce the scope of exemption.

As per the EACCMA 2004, some goods are prohibited and some restricted. "Prohibited goods" are the goods that cannot be imported

---

9   Major exemptions include: hotel equipment, unbleached woven fabrics, refrigerated trucks, insulated tankers, packaging materials for medicaments, items imported for use in licensed hospitals, diapers, urine bags and hygienic bags, horticulture, agriculture or floriculture inputs, specialised solar equipment and accessories, electrical energy saving bulbs for lighting, ships and other vessels, preparations for cleaning dairy apparatus, fish, and molluscs, containers and pallets, and imports by or on behalf of many privileged persons and institutions.

into any of the member states[10]. "Restricted goods" are those goods identified by the member states that need to be controlled by different government agencies[11]. These goods must meet certain conditions before clearance through customs. Import of these goods will only be granted against import permits, certificates or any other authority issued by respective agencies, providing or granting authority before import into the region. Some items have been declared as "sensitive items"[12], which are subject to higher import duties than the common external tariff.

6.3.2 Classification

It is necessary to develop a scientific and simple system of commodity classification. This would facilitate customs administration, leaving less scope for motivated interpretation and corruption. Besides, a scientific system of commodity classification is necessary for the compilation of accurate international trade statistics, which is necessary for the formulation of an appropriate economic policy in general and tax/trade policy in particular. An internationally accepted system of classification is more useful since it facilitates the compilation of internationally comparable data. Such a classification system is also necessary to levy different tariff rates on different commodities depending upon their nature. For example, the level of import duties depends upon the stages of development of a commodity in the EAC region, where raw materials are exempt, semi-processed goods are subject to moderate rates and final goods are subject to the highest import tariff. Hence goods must be classified in an appropriate manner according to their type, nature or stage of finish.

Currently, the internationally adopted commodity classification system is known as the Harmonised System, which was approved by the Customs Co-operation Council in June 1983 and is now applied by customs administration worldwide. EAC members also have adopted the Harmonised System, which is required to be adopted by the member

---

10   Examples of prohibited goods are: counterfeit currency notes and goods of all kinds, pornographic materials, matches containing white phosphorous, distilled beverages containing essential oils or chemical products, soaps and cosmetic products containing mercury and specified agricultural and industrial chemicals.

11   **Restricted goods include: p**ostal franking machines, arms and ammunition, bones and horn, ivory, elephant unworked or simply prepared but not cut to shape, ivory powder and waste, tortoise shell, whalebone and whalebone hair, horns etc., coral and similar materials, and natural sponges of animal origin.

12   These items include milk and cream, not converted nor containing added sugar or other sweetening matter, wheat and meslin flour, maize, cigars, cheroots and other tobacco products, cement, matches, specified fabrics, crown corks, and primary cells and primary batteries.

countries under the Protocol on the Establishment of the East African Customs Union. The EAC Harmonised System is organised into 21 sections and 97 chapters, where chapters 98 and 99 are reserved for special use of contracting parties and Chapter 77 is reserved for possible future use in the Harmonised System.

6.3.3. Tariff

EAC countries have to follow the EAC's rules regarding customs tariffs, which means no internal tariff can be levied on the import of goods produced within EAC member states. As stated earlier, the internal tariffs were eliminated in a phased manner over a period of 5 years when the Protocol on the Establishment of the East African Customs Union came into force.

Member states have to adopt a three band common external tariff in case of imports from outside the EAC region. The level of tariff depends upon the stage of finish of a product. For example, raw materials are subject to zero tariffs, semi-processed goods are subject to lower rates while the finished goods are subject to the higher tariff. The current common external tariffs are given in Table 6.1.

Table 6.1: Common External Tariffs

Items	Rates %
Raw materials, pharmaceuticals and capital goods, agricultural implements	0
Semi-finished goods	10
Final consumer goods or finished commercial goods	25

However, some items that have been specified as sensitive are subject to higher import duties than the above mentioned common external tariffs. For example, import duties applicable to some of the sensitive items are as follows:

Table 6.2: Import Tariffs on Selected Sensitive Items

Harmonised Code	Items	Rate
1001.90.20	Hard wheat	35
1005.90.00	Maize	50
1101.00.00	Wheat flour	60
2401.20.10	Cigars, cigarettes	35
2523.29.00	Cements	55

Harmonised Code	Items	Rate
3605.00.00	Matches	50
6302.31.00	Cotton bed linen	50
8309.10.00	Crown corks	40
8506.80.00	Other primary cells and primary batteries	35

Source: East African Community, Common External Tariff, 2007 Version, Schedule 2, pp.462-466.

The current rates of external tariff are expressed in *ad valorem* terms. However, in case of some sensitive items, such as paddy, rice, sugar, sacks and bags, and worn clothing and other worn articles, import duties are fixed on both specific and *ad valorem* basis and whichever is higher is the effective rate.[13]

6.4 Valuation

Customs duties are levied on the customs value, which includes all the cost associated with the imported goods up to the customs point. EAC member countries have adopted the WTO valuation system that focuses on the transaction value of imported goods, which is the price actually paid or payable, adjusted to include price paid for commissions and brokerages except buying commission, cost of containers, packaging, transport, loading, unloading and handling charges, insurance, and royalties.[14]

If it is not possible to establish transaction value in this way, then only[15] customs value may be established on the basis of the five alternative valuation methods, which are: transaction value of identical goods, transaction value of similar goods, deductive method, computed method and fall back method. These methods should be applied strictly in sequential order but not concurrently. For example, if the customs

---

13   For example, in case of paddy and rice, customs duties are fixed at 75% or USD 200 MT, whichever is higher. In case of sugar, the corresponding rate is 100% or USD 200/MT whichever is higher. In case of sacks and bags, import duties are levied at 45% or USD 0.45/ bag, whichever is higher. Worn clothing and other worn articles are subject to 45% or USD 0.30/kg, whichever is higher.
14   For details see Paragraphs 2 and 9 of Schedule IV of the EACCMA 2004.
15   While customs duties have been levied on customs value, which is the total of cost, insurance and freight (CIF), due to the general problems of the lack of proper invoices, there have been practices in different countries to levy customs duties on arbitrary or fictitious customs values which are artificially fixed by the customs officials or the customs valuation committees. This has been a source of collusion, corruption and revenue leakage in many customs administrations.

value cannot be established using the transaction value method, then the customs value will be the transaction value of identical goods[16] imported by the partner state at or around the same time as goods being valued at the same commercial level in the same quantity. If the customs value cannot be determined on the basis of transaction value or transaction value of identical goods, then the customs value will be the transaction value of similar goods[17] which are imported around the same time in the same commercial level and in the same quantity.

Similarly, if the customs value cannot be established on the basis of the methods mentioned above, then it will be determined by using the deductive method, which is obtained by deducting from selling price the commission, travel and in transport cost and customs duties etc. Likewise, when the customs value cannot be determined on the basis of the previously mentioned methods, it will be calculated on the basis of the computed method. Under this method, customs value is obtained by adding the cost of production plus general expenses up to border and profit. On the other hand, if customs value cannot be determined by using any other method, then it should be determined using reasonable means, generally based on the previously determined values and methods.

Valuation is one of the important aspects of the customs administration. It will remain important even when customs duties are reduced substantially and their relative importance as a revenue raiser or protective measure reduces drastically. This is because VAT and excise duties on imports are levied on customs value. So in order to levy these taxes properly, it is necessary to have proper valuation.

---

16   EACCMA 2004 defines identical goods as "goods, which are same in all respects, including physical characteristics, quality and reputation. Minor differences in appearance shall not preclude goods otherwise conforming to the definition from being regarded as identical."

17   Similar goods are defined as "goods, which although not alike in all aspects, have like characteristics and like component materials which enable them to perform the same functions and to be commercially interchangeable. The quality of the goods, their reputation and the existence of a trademark are among the factors to be considered in determining whether goods are similar."

Besides, proper valuation is important for non-revenue measures, which are stated in *A Handbook on WTO Customs Valuation Agreement*[18] as follows:

- Import quotas based on customs value.
- Rules of origin. For example, a country may allow goods from a specific foreign country to enter free of duty if 50% of the customs value of the import is contributed by operations carried out in that foreign country.
- Collection of trade statistics.

For the purposes of customs valuation, it is common to use the official exchange rate posted by the central bank.

6.5 Pre-shipment inspection

While as mentioned above the proper customs valuation is important for several reasons, many developing countries face valuation problems, where under valuation of imported goods is the rule rather than the exception. These countries often lack information on prices of varieties of imported goods to challenge undervaluation of these goods. In this context, Kenya, Rwanda, Tanzania and Uganda are making limited use of the service of Pre-Shipment Inspection (PSI) companies to address the customs valuation problem.

PSI companies inspect goods to be imported and set their valuation and classification before they enter the country. They are involved in the supervision of the loading and sealing of containers and provide intelligence information on suspected or actual fraud. They also provide experts, conduct training, and produce periodic reports to the customs/Ministry of Finance. PSI companies also help prevent the import of goods that are harmful to health. They are, in fact, involved in a variety of activities regarding the import of goods such as verification of quantity, inspection of quality, determination of price, checking of classification and reviewing currency exchange rates. These activities of PSI companies help improve the valuation and classification of goods, reduce the compliance and administration costs of international trade, check collusion and corruption in the customs administration, control revenue leakage and enhance revenue collection. PSI programs also make it possible to reduce the level of tariffs without a corresponding reduction in the customs revenue collection. Lower tariffs, on the

---

18   Sheri Rosenow & Brain J. O'Shea, *A Handbook on WTO Customs Valuation Agreement*, World Trade Organization, December 2010, p.4.

other hand, are considered more efficient, both economically and administratively, than the higher ones.

However, PSI companies' presence itself does not guarantee the success of the PSI programs. There are cases of both success and failure of PSI programs. The degree of success depends upon the design and administration, relation between the customs administration and PSI companies, customs administration's willingness to make use of the information provided by the PSI companies, and attitude, integrity and efficiency of the PSI company staff that are involved in the implementation of PSI program of a country concerned. The trading community does not support PSI fully anyway.

6.6 Post clearance audit

While trade facilitation is a very important task of the modern customs administration, it is also crucial to "control the cross-border flow of goods, ensure compliance with government rules and regulations ... and protect the country against the import of goods and materials intended for illegal purposes, and against terrorist activities."[19] Thus the modern customs administrations "face the challenge of facilitating the movement of legitimate passengers and cargo while applying controls to detect Customs fraud and other offences."[20] There is a need to maintain a reasonable balance between the facilitation of legitimate trade and control of illicit activities.

In the light of the increasing volume of international trade, it is neither possible nor desirable to run customs under the traditional 100% physical control system where all goods, vehicles or passengers are examined. Such a system causes delays, hinders trade, opens scope for harassment, collusion and corruption and increases the cost of doing business. On the other hand, under such a system, as goods are supposed to be checked by customs officials before they are released, importers do not feel solely responsible for any wrong doing relating to classification and/or valuation of goods and try to misclassify goods or manipulate their values with or without collusion with customs officials. Besides, customs officials may not have full understanding of a transaction and may not be able to resolve classification/valuation or any

---

19   UNCTAD Trust Fund for Trade Facilitation Negotiations Technical Note No. 3, Use of Customs Automation Systems, p.2.

20   UNCTAD Trust Fund on Trade Facilitation Negotiations, Technical Note No. 12, Risk Management For Customs Control, Produced jointly by the World Customs Organization (WCO) and UNCTAD, p.1.

other issues properly at the customs point due to the lack of necessary documentation.

So these days focus has shifted from 100% physical checks to the risk management–based cargo selectivity system, where the level of customs intervention depends upon revenue risk and intelligence. In some cases, physical check of goods at the customs points is replaced by the audit based control that is carried out at the trader's premises. For example, under the Automated System for Customs Data (ASYCUDA) system, which is discussed shortly, customs control is maintained by using risk management tools as follows:[21]

Channel	Customs Control
Green Channel	Immediate release without examination
Yellow Channel	Documentary check
Red Channel	Physical examination of goods and documents
Blue Channel	Examination at a later stage (post clearance audit-PCA)

The modern approach is to scrutinise high-risk imports and to allow low-risk imports to pass customs without any customs intervention. Similarly, imports flagged for post-clearance audit also pass customs without any check.[22] But they are subject to audit at the trader's premises, which is carried out "to verify the accuracy and authenticity of declarations and covers the control of traders' commercial data, business systems, records and books."[23] PCA allows customs officers to resolve concerns about correct reporting of value, classification, rate of duty, and country of origin in flagged declarations.[24]

PCA is beneficial for the traders as well as the customs administration. As PCA is carried out at the trader's premises, goods are subject to fewer interventions at the import point, which reduces delay in the clearance of goods and saves payment of warehouse charges. PCA

---

21   UNCTAD Trust Fund on Trade Facilitation Negotiations, Technical Note No. 12, Risk Management For Customs Control, Produced jointly by the World Customs Organization (WCO) and UNCTAD, p.2.

22   United States Agency for International Development, *Customs Modernization Handbook*, Post-Clearance Audit Program, A Businesslike Approach To Customs Control, Produced by Nathan Associates Inc. for the United States Agency for International Development, October 2011, p.4.

23   UNCTAD Trust Fund on Trade Facilitation Negotiations, Technical Note No. 5, Post-Clearance Audit, Produced jointly by the World Customs Organization (WCO) and UNCTAD, p.1.

24   United States Agency for International Development, *op. cit.*, p.4.

may be instrumental in raising the level of voluntary compliance among the traders and "detect or prevent fraud."[25] Because of this, PCA has been adopted by EAC member states also and the EAC Secretariat has published a PCA manual that sets out guidelines and spells out in detail the process of conducting PCA.[26]

6.7 Automation

Automation is crucial for an efficient and effective running of the customs administration as it:

- facilitates day to day work of the customs administration,
- saves time and costs of both the customs administration and traders,
- expedites processing of customs documents,
- brings transparency in the customs administration,
- minimises the scope for collusion and corruption since it reduces the need of physical contact between the customs officials and traders,
- helps customs administration to "store vast amounts of data in a single electronic database and reduces storage costs."[27]

That is why there is an increasing trend around the world to automate customs administrations and EAC customs administrations are not exceptions.

Of the EAC countries, Burundi, Rwanda, Tanzania and Uganda have adopted ASYCUDA, which is a computerised system designed by the United Nations Conference on Trade and Development (UNCTAD) to administer customs. It "is an automated Customs data management system that can handle all Customs clearance-related processes."[28] ASYCUDA system was first developed in 1981 for West African Countries to compile their foreign trade statistics. The system was upgraded over the years. For example, while ASYCYDA ++[29] was introduced in 1992, ASYCUDA World[30] was adopted in 2002. ASYCUDA has

---

25   *Ibid.*, p.1.

26   East African Community, *Customs Post Clearance Audit Manual*, EAC Secretariat, Arusha, January 2012.

27   Parthasarathi Shome, *Tax Shastra, Administrative Reforms in India, United Kingdom and Brazil*, BS Books, New Delhi, 2012, p.74.

28   UNCTAD Trust Fund for Trade Facilitation Negotiations Technical Note No. 21, Automated System for Customs Data (ASYCUDA), p.1.

29   ASYCUDA ++ included new customs modules and functionalities such as direct trader input, risk management, transit monitoring and submissions of declarations by Customs brokers via the Internet. See UNCTAD Trust Fund for Trade Facilitation Negotiations Technical Note No. 21, Automated System for Customs Data (ASYCUDA), p.1.

30   This is considered as a truly e-Customs version that is compatible with major database management and operating systems. See UNCTAD Trust Fund for Trade Facilitation

been spreading around the world due to its several benefits,[31] and has already been adopted by more than 90 countries. As the system allows for direct trader input, importers can lodge declarations from their premises, which reduces clearance time. ASYCUDA has also been used to generate trade statistics which are exported to an ORACLE database used to convert the data into formats such as Excel and Access.[32] On the other hand, Kenya adopted SIMBA,[33] which is an online customs clearance system that is going to be replaced by a new system in 2015.[34]

6.8 Mechanism to make export duty free

EAC member countries have adopted various schemes to encourage exports, including export processing zone (EPZ), bonded warehouse, and duty drawback. As goods benefiting from export promotion schemes are primarily meant for export, they will be subject to full duties, and taxes provided for in the common external tariff if they are sold in the community.

6.8.1 Export Processing Zone

An EPZ is a designated area, which is generally located near a harbour or international transport point. Under the EACCMA 2004, it is necessary to obtain permission of the Commissioner of the Customs to carry on any activity in an EPZ. Firms established in the EPZ have to maintain records of plant, machinery and equipment, raw materials and goods manufactured in the EPZ. They can import plant, machinery, equipment and materials such as raw materials, supplementary raw materials, chemicals, fuel, and packaging materials for the manufacture of export goods under security, without payment of duty/taxes. If duty/tax free imported goods/materials are sold in the local market or used to produce goods to be sold in the home market, the customs duties and

---

Negotiations Technical Note No. 21, Automated System for Customs Data (ASYCUDA), p.1.

31   Potential direct benefits of ASYCUDA are "faster processing of declarations and thus clearance, more efficient controls, accurate and detailed accounting, increased revenue and accurate and timely data on external trade." See ASYCUDA, Automated System for Customs Data, ASYCUDA ++ Description of Application Software (Technical Overview), United Nations Conference on Trade and Development, p.2.

32   African Development Bank Group, *Domestic Resource Mobilization for Poverty Reduction in East Africa: Burundi Case Study*, Regional Development East A (OREA), November 2010, p.13.

33   SIMBA was introduced in July 2005 in place of the Bishops Office Freight Forwarders Integrated Network (BOFFIN) system that was in operation since 1989.

34   See http://www.capitalfm.co.ke/business/2013/11/kra-to-replace-simba-system-by-2015/.

other taxes to be collected at the point of import will be collected from the concerned industry.

Since no tax is imposed on the materials imported for EPZs and there is not much interference by the employees of customs/tax administration, the EPZ system promotes exports. It also holds special importance in attracting foreign investment since foreign investors do not have to come in contact with the local administration under the EPZ system. Other benefits of operating such a system include free trade conditions, streamlined government red tape allowing for one stop registration and licensing and also a facility of long term tax concession.

6.8.2 Bonded Warehouse

Like EPZ, the system of bonded warehouse also allows an industry to import plant, machinery, equipment and materials for the manufacture of exports under a bond, without payment of duty/taxes on imports. However, unlike EPZ, where an industry has to be located in the designed area, under the bonded warehouse system an industry/warehouse can be established in any area. It is, however, necessary under the EACCMA 2004 to obtain a license from the Commissioner of Customs to operate a bonded warehouse, which remains valid until the end of the year. Operators of a bonded warehouse have to provide details of the physical facility of the bonded warehouse to the Commissioner of Customs and record details of imported items under the bond and provide such information to the concerned officials at the time of inspection. If the imported materials are sold in the local market, customs duties and other taxes will be imposed on raw materials/equipment that were imported under the bond without paying duties and taxes.

It is, however, not easy to operate a bonded warehouse system as it is difficult to estimate the customs duties/taxes since some of the imported or purchased materials are used to produce goods for export products and some are not. Similarly, machinery and equipment may be used for a long time in future and it cannot be determined whether these goods will be exported in future. The imported raw materials may also be used for the production of goods to be supplied inside the country. Hence, bonded warehouse facilities are prone to misuse. To minimise the possibility of misuse, some conditions as follows may be fixed to make someone eligible to obtain a license to operate a bonded warehouse:

- who produce goods only for export,
- who export more than a certain percentage of the total production, or
- who export more than a fixed amount.

6.8.3 Duty Draw Back

Under the duty draw back system, exporters get back the customs duty paid on the import of raw materials, auxiliary raw materials, packaging materials, chemicals, machinery, equipment, fuel, etc. that are used to produce exports. According to the EACCMA 2004, duty drawback may be allowed on goods imported for use in the manufacturing of goods which are exported or transferred to a free port or an EPZ. In order to avail this facility, a manufacturer must obtain an authorisation from the Commissioner of Customs prior to manufacture of the goods. The commissioner has to fix or agree to the rate of yield of the operations and prescribe applicable duty drawback coefficient. A manufacturer has to prepare the list of goods and produce the goods for examination by the proper officer before export or transfer to a free port or an EPZ. Claim for drawback must be made with 12 months from the date of export of goods or the transfer to the free port or an EPZ.

Like the bonded warehouse system, it is not easy to operate the duty drawback system. It is difficult to estimate customs on parts of the inputs that are used to produce only exports since some of the materials are used for export products and some are not. Similarly, machinery and equipment may be used to produce goods for a long time in future and it cannot be determined whether or not those goods will be exported in future. The imported raw materials may also be used for the production of goods to be sold inside the country. Effective monitoring is required in order to curb misuse of the system.

Much accounting is required to estimate the customs duties/taxes imposed on inputs of exports. In some countries tax is refunded on the basis of input-output coefficient and in others an average rate is maintained for administrative simplicity. The system of maintaining an average rate results in inequity – some might get a higher amount and some less than duty paid – since the exporters do not get the refund on the basis of the amount of duty paid.

It is believed that there is some over spill of commodity taxation into exports which detracts from the competitive power of domestic products in the international market. It is, therefore, necessary to make tax refund and duty drawback system effective in order to relieve exports from the burden of commodity taxation.

6.9 Customs agents

The EACCM Act, 2004 authorises the Commissioner of the Customs to issue a license to the customs agent to clear goods through customs on behalf of the owners of goods. A Customs Agent license is provided for one calendar year, which expires on the 31st December of every year. Customs agents need to be knowledgeable about customs clearance procedures.

The owner of the goods may authorise the customs agent in writing either generally or in relation to any particular consignment to perform the work on his behalf. He should provide the agent the relevant documents in unaltered state and equip the agent with a true and correct position to avoid misrepresentation. A customs agent may be appointed by more than one person as their agent and the agent must notify the Commissioner that he intends to act on behalf of various clients who have authorised him to do so.

The authorised customs agent will be deemed as the owner of the goods and will be liable for the payment of duties/taxes. He will be responsible for preparing and presenting the declarations to Customs. The agent may also sign any other documents on behalf of his client on request. The agent will make sure that all taxes due are paid as required on the consignments he handles on behalf of the owner of the goods. However, the owner of the goods also will remain responsible for the payment of duties/taxes on the importation/exportation of goods.

6.10 Summary

While customs duties have traditionally been important sources of government revenues in the EAC region, their relative importance in the total tax structure has been reducing gradually due to the development of domestic trade taxes and income taxes, and also due to the move towards a more liberal trade policy and, as indicated earlier in Section 1.5, now these duties provide only about 8% of total tax revenue. EAC countries have established a customs union, adopted a common customs law and harmonised customs procedures. They have adopted the harmonised system of commodity classification and a common exemption policy. While internal tariffs have been dismantled on the import of goods produced in the EAC region, a 3-tier external tariff structure has been fixed at 0%, 10% and 25% on goods imported from outside EAC region.

However, EAC member states levy high import duties on many sensitive items. As stated earlier, high rates are costly, both economically and administratively and reduce competitiveness of the goods produced in the EAC region in the international market. On the other hand, there are large exemptions that not only reduce the tax base and revenue but also cause delay, disputes, harassment, collusion, and corruption. This warrants the removal of exemptions except ones provided under the international agreements. This would lead to an expansion in customs coverage and would make it possible to lower tariffs without reducing customs revenue and reduce both the administrative and economic costs of the import duties.

Chapter 7

Inter-Governmental Fiscal Relations

7.1 Introduction

There are two systems of government: unitary and federal. The unitary system consists of two tiers of government vis., national and local; the federal system has three layers vis., national, state and local. Local governments again can have one or more layers. National governments are also referred to as federal or central governments, whereas state and local governments are known as sub-national governments.[1] While different levels of governments have some independent as well as shared decision making responsibilities under the federal system, effective control of all government functions rests with the national government under the unitary system.[2]

Both the national and sub-national governments are assigned expenditure responsibilities and authorities for taxation. Of the three major functions for the public sector – macroeconomic stabilisation, income distribution and resource allocation – traditional theory of fiscal federalism assigns stabilisation and redistribution functions mainly to the national government, while allocation function largely rests with the

1   "Sub-national governments" refer to all levels of government below the national level.
2   Robin Boadway and Anwar Shah, *Fiscal Federalism, Principles and Practices of Multiorder Governance*, Cambridge University Press, 2009, pp.4-5.

sub-national governments. As Musgrave observes, "The heart of fiscal federalism thus lies in the proposition that the policies of the Allocation Branch should be permitted to differ between states, depending on the preferences of their citizens. The objectives of the Distribution and Stabilisation Branches require primary responsibility at the central level."[3]

The stabilisation function is basically assigned to the national government that is responsible for maintaining macro-economic stability in the country by means of a set of fiscal and monetary policies, such as imposition of broad-based taxes, borrowing or printing money. National governments also attempt to maintain macro-economic stability through major expenditure programs. On the other hand, sub-national governments often lack the necessary macroeconomic tools to carry out economic stabilisation policies[4] and have no or little incentive to implement such policies as their impact is believed to spill out of their jurisdictions.[5]

Similarly, the distribution function is also primarily assigned to the national government. This function "involves the role of government in changing the distribution of income, wealth or other indicators of economic well-being to make them more equitable than would otherwise be the case."[6] This can be done by implementing broad-based progressive taxes by the national government, which if levied with high rates by the sub-national governments, may drive out high income individuals as they would have to bear high tax liability,[7] defeating the objective of progressive taxes. Similarly, "expenditures undertaken by government for equity or income equalisation reasons, such as social welfare or low income housing is generally thought to be the domain of the central government. Local or regional governments will not be able to sustain independent programs of this nature because they will attract

---

3   Richard A. Musgrave, *The Theory of Public Finance, A Study in Public Economy*, McGraw-Hill Book Company, New York, Toronto and London, Inc., 1959, pp.181-182.

4   Wallace E. Oates, "An Essay on Fiscal Federalism", *Journal of Economic Literature*, Vol. XXXVII, September 1999, p.1121.

5   Charles E. McLure and Jorge Martinez-Vazquez, The Assignment of Revenues and Expenditures in Intergovernmental Fiscal Relations, p.3, World Bank Institute's Decentralization Homepage (www.worldbank.org/decentralization).

6   James Edwin Kee, *Fiscal Decentralization: Theory as Reform*, VIII Congreso International del CLAD sobre la Reforma del Estado Y de la Administración Publica, Panama, 28-31 Oct. 2003, p.2.

7   Wallace E. Oates, *op. cit.*, p.1121.

the needy from other areas while they will have to tax their (potentially mobile) residents more heavily."[8]

On the other hand, allocation function, which is the delivery of goods and services by the government, may be assigned to both the national and sub-national governments as "each level of government may be more efficient in delivering certain governmental goods and services."[9] The Tiebout model indicates that as highly mobile households "choose as a jurisdiction of residence that locality that provides the fiscal package best suited to their tastes,"[10] local governments can provide some goods and services efficiently in their areas. Tiebout observes: "Given these revenue and expenditure patterns, the consumer-voter moves to that community whose local government best satisfies his set of preferences. The greater the number of communities and the greater the variance among them, the closer the consumer will come to fully realizing his preference position."[11]

In practice, countries differ in terms of assignment of expenditure and revenue responsibilities to various levels of government. Besides, the level of services provided by various levels of government to their citizen and revenue received by them from their citizens is also affected by the degree of implementation of both revenue and expenditure responsibilities.

As discussed later, most buoyant taxes are more efficiently and equitably administered at the national level, while many of the more costly services are better administered at the sub-national level. This leads to vertical imbalance. On the other hand, unequal location of the revenue sources amongst the sub-national governments, their differential ability to mobilise revenues from these sources, their differential expenditure needs, the different costs of service provision and their differential ability to provide these services lead to horizontal imbalance. These fiscal imbalances are corrected by means of inter-governmental transfers.

In this chapter, we examine inter-governmental fiscal relationships that reflect the respective assignment of expenditure and revenue responsibilities between the national and sub-national

---

8   Charles E. McLure & Jorge Martinez-Vazquez, *op. cit*, p.6.
9   James Edwin Kee, *op. cit.*, p.2.
10   Wallace E. Oates, *op. cit.*, p.1124.
11   Charles M. Tiebout, A Pure Theory of Local Expenditures. *The Journal of Political Economy*, 64, 5, October 1956, pp.418.

governments, and the inter-governmental transfer system in the EAC region.

7.2. System of government

All the EAC member states have adopted the unitary system of government, where there are two tiers of government; vis.; national and local level governments as given below:

Table 7.1: Type and Tiers of Government in the EAC Countries

Country	Type of Government	Tiers of Government
Burundi	Unitary	National and Local
Kenya	Unitary	National and Local
Rwanda	Unitary	National and Local
Tanzania	Unitary	National and Local
Uganda	Unitary	National and Local

EAC countries have made constitutional provision for local governments, which, however, is brief in some countries while detailed in others.[12] For example, the Rwanda Constitution simply states that the number, boundaries, organisation and functions of the local bodies will be determined by an Organic Law. On the other hand, the Ugandan Constitution makes a detailed provision relating to local governments.[13]

Local governments are governed under a separate act in each of the EAC countries. For example, local governments operate under the Local Government Act 1977 in Kenya, the Rwanda Organic Law No. 29 of 2005 in Rwanda, Local Governments Act 1997 in Uganda, and Local Government (District Authorities) Act 1982 in case of rural areas and the Local Government (Urban Authorities) Act 1982 in case of urban areas in Tanzania.[14] Local governments are structured in different ways in these countries. For example, while the local government in the rural areas in Kenya is single tiered, Uganda has a multi-tier government system.[15]

---

12   See Article 3 of Rwandan Constitution, Articles 176-207 of Ugandan Constitution,
      Articles 145 and 146 of Tanzanian Constitution, and Article 176 of Kenyan Constitution.
13   Chapter 11 of the Uganda constitution is dedicated to the local government and deals
      with various aspects, including boundaries, elections, authorities, staffing, functions, tax
      power and grants system of the local governments.
14   Other related laws are: Local Government Finances Act 1982 and Urban Authorities
      Rating Act 1983.
15   In Uganda, a village/ward is the lowest tier of local government. Several villages/wards
      make up a Parish while several Parishes make up a sub-country/town and several sub-

Table 7.2: Structure of Local Governments in the EAC Countries

Country	Forms of Local Government
Burundi	Provinces and communes
Kenya	Rural areas: Counties Urban areas: Towns, Municipalities, and Cities
Rwanda	Villages, Cells, Sectors and Districts
Tanzania	Rural areas: Vitongoji/Hamlets, Villages and Districts Urban areas: Municipalities, Towns and Cities
Uganda	Rural area: Villages, Parishes, Sub-counties, Counties, and Districts Urban areas: Wards, Towns, Municipalities, and Cities

7.3 Expenditure responsibilities assignment

Different levels of governments are assigned different expenditure responsibilities. While some responsibilities are handled exclusively by one level of government, others are carried out by different levels of government, albeit with different degrees. For example, while matters of national and international importance such as national defence and foreign affairs are inherently handled by the national government, local governments are generally responsible for such locality-specific issues as garbage collection, street cleaning and beautification of local areas. Some activities such as education, health, and roads are managed by different levels of government on different scales. Expenditure responsibilities of various levels of government are included in the constitutions of some countries,[16] but they are governed by other laws in other countries.

---

counties/towns make up one county/municipality. A district/city is the highest tier of local government, which is made up of a number of counties/municipalities.

16   For example, Article185 (2), 186 (1) and 187 (2)) and Schedule IV of the Constitution of Kenya.

While different levels of government may have different expenditure responsibilities in different countries, in general, an indicative assignment of responsibilities between various levels of governments is as follows:

Table 7.3: Indicative Assignment of Expenditure Responsibilities between Levels of Governments

National	State	Local
Defence	Local Government oversight	Garbage collection
Foreign affairs		Street lighting
Border control	State land and state natural resources	Town planning
Quarantine		Building approvals
Immigration/emigration	Health care	Primary health care
Naturalisation and citizenship	Education	Primary education
Airports and air safety	Registration of marriage, divorce, inheritance, birth, death, adoption and affiliations	Trees and footpaths
International treaties and policies		Community facilities
Monetary policy, banking and currency		Domestic animals
Social security/pensions	Intrastate public transport and roads	Fire control and ambulance services
Healthcare	State public utilities	
Education	Vehicle licensing, issuance of driving licenses and number plates	
Postal services		
Telecommunications and broadcasting		
Industrial relations	Regional infrastructure	
International/interstate trade	Inter-local jurisdiction matters	

Sources: Anwar Shah, *The Reform of Intergovernmental Fiscal Relations in Developing and Emerging Market Economies*, The World Bank, Washington DC, 1994, p.12 and Robin Boadway and Anwar Shah, *Fiscal Federalism, Principles and Practices of Multi-order Governance*, Cambridge University Press, 2009, pp.134-135.

As stated above, such functions as national defence, foreign affairs, border controls and immigration are under the domain of the national government. Similarly, programs operated to stabilise the economy such as massive investment, or unemployment compensation and social welfare programs run for equity or income equalisation reasons belong to the national government.[17] Such services as garbage collection,

---

17   Nina Boschmann, Development Partners Working Group on Local Governance and Decentralization DPWG-LGD, Fiscal Decentralization and Options for Donor Harmonization, December 2009, p.33.

street cleaning, street/traffic lighting and primary education could be managed better by the local governments. The bottom line is that "a local government is best placed to deliver those services for which the delivery area falls entirely within the administrative boundaries of that government unit,"[18] while activities that may spill over to other jurisdictions can be managed better by the higher level of government.[19] Some functions may be shared between two or more levels of governments. In such cases, the national government should be responsible for overall policies, setting standards and auditing. Intermediate governments are responsible for overseeing implementation and local governments for the delivery of services.[20] It is desirable to shape welfare programs at the central level, but execute locally, with some discretion, e.g. discerning who is really eligible and who only pretends to be. These and housing programs simply cannot be executed by the central level in a large country. In some cases, responsibilities may specifically be distributed between various levels of governments. For example, in the case of education, national government can better manage education standards and curriculum development, state government can better handle higher education and the local governments can better run primary education.

In practice, scope of responsibilities of different levels of governments varies from country to country and in a country over a period of time, depending upon the degree of centralisation/decentralisation. Under the centralised system, authority is concentrated in the hands of the national government. Local governments have limited autonomy and responsibilities, which work under the "principal-agent" model, where "the principal (the central government) may alter jurisdictional boundaries, local government revenue and expenditure responsibilities"[21] of the local governments and the agent (local government), "...serves at the central government's behest or at its instruction." Local government may be elected, but it has so few powers or authorities as to make it incapable of providing services other than those mandated and funded by the central government."[22] Thus the

18   *Ibid.*, p.33.
19   For the roles and responsibilities of various levels of government with special reference to the middle level government see Horst Zimmermann, *Roles versus functions for the federal middle level: A structure and a growth perspective*, Working Paper Series No.1, Faculty of Economics, Toyo University, Tokyo, January 2011.
20   Jorge Martinez-Vazquez, Andrey Timofeev, and Jameson Boex, *Reforming Regional-Local Finance in Russia*, The World Bank, 2006, p.58.
21   Richard M. Bird, "Threading the Fiscal Labyrinth: Some Issues in Fiscal Decentralization," *National Tax Journal* Vol. 46, No. 2, June, 1993, p.209.
22   Nina Boschmann, *op. cit.*, p.24.

national governments generally treat the sub-national governments as their agents in implementing national policies.[23] Rationale for the centralisation is that there is limited administrative capacity to carry out both the expenditure and revenue responsibilities at the local level in the developing and transitional countries. Besides, decentralisation might increase the possibility for corruption due to the increase in the number of public positions and it becomes more difficult to administer a large number of decentralised offices than a lower number of centralised offices.[24]

There has, however, been increasing focus on fiscal decentralisation in different countries during the last two decades or so, which is "the devolution of taxing and spending powers to lower levels of government."[25] The reason for the increased decentralisation is the "principle of subsidiarity", according to which public authority should reside at the lowest level of political organisation capable of using it effectively. As local governments are closer to the people they can respond more quickly and appropriately to changing local conditions than can the national government,[26] there is a possibility for a better match of supply and demand for public goods through local services[27] and close satisfaction of individual preferences. It is true that one size will not fit all, i.e. "consumers' preferences differ within a county; and, therefore, (the idea of) uniform levels of services in all municipalities is inefficient. In this sense, decentralized service delivery increases efficiency, as services can be provided according to local preferences."[28] This means that local governments can provide public services in their "benefit area" more efficiently. Besides, decentralisation makes local governments more accountable for their actions. It is also likely to promote democracy. "Finally, fiscal decentralization is thought to enhance political participation at the local level. This has the potential

23   The United Republic of Tanzania President's Office, Final Report: Developing a System of Inter-governmental Grants in Tanzania, A report prepared for Local Government Reform Program by Georgia State University Andrew Young School of Public Policy, January 31, 2003, p.98.

24   Daniel P. Hewitt, "Transfers to Local Government," in Ke-young Chu and Richard Hemming edits. *Public Expenditure Handbook, A Guide to Public Expenditure Policy Issues in Developing Countries*, Government Expenditure Analysis Division, Fiscal Affairs Department, International Monetary Fund, Washington DC, 1991, p.84.

25   Odd-Helge Fjeldstad, *Intergovernmental Fiscal Relations in Developing Countries: A Review of Issues*, WP 2001:11, Chr. Michelsen Institute Development Studies and Human Rights, p.2.

26   *Ibid.*, p.2.

27   *Ibid.*, p.1.

28   Nina Boschmann, *op. cit.*, p.23.

to enhance democratic values and political stability at the local level. It provides a forum for local debate about local priorities, and can be a proving ground for future political leaders."[29]

Regarding appropriate assignment of expenditure responsibilities between the national and sub-national governments, Bird states that the "basic rule of efficient expenditure assignment is to assign each function to the lowest level of government consistent with its efficient performance. So long as there are local variations in tastes and costs, there are clearly efficiency gains from carrying out public sector activities in as decentralised a fashion as possible. The only services that should be provided centrally are those for which there are no differences in demands in different localities, where there are substantial spill-overs between jurisdictions that cannot be handled in some other way (e.g., by contracting or by grant design), or for which the additional costs of local administration are sufficiently higher to outweigh its advantages."[30]

In the EAC region also there has been an increasing focus on fiscal decentralisation since the 1980s. Ugandan decentralisation efforts are considered a successful example in Africa.[31] As stated earlier, the Ugandan constitution makes detailed provisions regarding local governments. It is stated therein that decentralisation is a principle applicable to all levels of local governments and, in particular, from higher to lower local government units to ensure peoples' participation and democratic control in decision making. It also mentions that the system shall be such as to ensure that functions, powers and responsibilities are devolved and transferred from the national government to local government units in a coordinated manner.[32] Here, the overriding goal, since decentralisation was conceived in 1986,[33] has been to bring services (government) closer to the people. As stated later, the Ugandan grant system reflects the devolution of functions as the grants are reckoned annually with reference to the reassignment of tasks between the national and sub-national governments.

Local governments were reintroduced in Tanzania in 1984 and a local government reform program was initiated in 1999.[34] Local governments are established in each region, district, urban area and village to transfer

---

29   James Edwin Kee, *op. cit.*, p.3.
30   Richard M. Bird, *op. cit.*, p.210.
31   The United Republic of Tanzania President's Office, *op. cit.*, p.137.
32   Article 176 of Ugandan Constitution.
33   Republic of Uganda, Local Government Finance Commission, Introduction of Equalization Grant, Analysis and Recommendations, March 1999, p.1.
34   The United Republic of Tanzania President's Office, *op. cit.*, p.3-4.

authority to the people. Local government authorities have the right and power to participate and to involve the people, in the planning and implementation of development programs in their respective areas.

Kenya has given high priority to decentralisation where the functions of the national and local governments are clearly demarcated in the Constitution. As indicated in Appendix 7a, county governments have been authorised to carry out many public functions, including control of air pollution and noise pollution, county public works and services, county health services, county transport, and implementation of specific national government policies on natural resources and environmental conservation.

7.4. Tax assignment

Revenue sources are assigned to the national and sub-national governments to provide revenues to carry out their functions. A major source of government revenue is taxation. It is necessary to identify which taxes are appropriate to be levied at what level. In this context, one should keep in mind which taxes match the major responsibilities of a particular level of government. For example, as stabilisation and distribution functions are basically national government functions, "tax instruments that can significantly affect macroeconomic stabilization and income redistribution should be assigned to the central government."[35]

---

35   Jorge Martinez-Vazquez, Andrey Timofeev, and Jameson Boex, *op. cit.*, p.81.

Regarding the assignment of taxes between various levels of governments, the following 'tax-assignment rules' have been developed in the traditional theory of fiscal federalism:[36]

National level
- Taxes suitable for economic stabilisation
- Progressive re-distributional taxes
- Tax bases distributed highly unequally between jurisdictions
- Taxes difficult to administer and easy to evade

Sub-national level
- Taxes that have bases with low mobility between jurisdictions
- Cyclically stable taxes
- Benefit taxes

National and sub-national level
- User charges

An indicative assignment of taxes between the levels of government may be stated as follows:

Table 7.4: Indicative Assignment of Taxes between the Levels of Governments

National	State	Local
Exclusive taxes		
Customs duties	PIT (piggy-backing)	Real estate property taxes
BPT	Presumptive tax	Entertainment tax
PIT	Stamp duties	Cattle tax
Natural resource taxes	Registration fees	Tolls
Social security contributions	Vehicle tax	User charges
Carbon taxes	Gambling/lottery taxes	
User charges	User charges	
Shared taxes		
VAT	VAT	
Excise duties	Excise duties	

---

36   Robin Boadway and Anwar Shah, *op. cit.*, pp.91-92; and Odd-Helge Fjeldstad, *op. cit.*, p.6.

Customs duties:

Customs duties are universally levied by the national government on goods crossing international boundaries. While customs duties-like "internal duties" used to be levied by sub-national governments on the internal movement of goods in the past in some countries, they have been abandoned in modern times as they hinder the free flow of goods and impede trade and commerce. That is why even constitutions of some countries prohibit sub-national governments from levying taxes on the internal movement of goods. For example, Article 121 of the Constitution Act 1867 of Canada establishes the principle that the governments will allow the free internal movements of goods, which means that no internal customs duties will be permitted on the internal movement of goods.[37] Article 301 of the Indian Constitution advocates for free flow of goods within the country. This has also been recognised in East Africa. For example, Kenya's Constitution states that the taxation and other revenue-raising powers of a county shall not be exercised in a way that prejudices national economic policies, economic activities across county boundaries or the national mobility of goods, services, capital or labour.

VAT:

VAT is basically a national level tax. If it is levied at the sub-national level with different structures in different tax jurisdictions, resources may be diverted from the high taxed to the low taxed jurisdictions. This would also raise the compliance costs of the taxpayers as they would have to study various tax laws adopted by different tax jurisdictions and follow different procedures if they have operation in multiple tax jurisdictions. Further, "VATs are ideally suited for jurisdictions that have border controls. The absence of such controls between states makes the administration of a fully decentralized VAT system almost nonviable."[38] In addition, such a tax is likely to be exported outside tax jurisdiction which is not in line with the principle of non-exportability of the burden of sub-national tax. Thus it is better to levy this type of tax at the national level with a nationwide uniform structure and procedures. That is why this tax, with a few exceptions, is levied by the national governments all over the world, including in many federal countries. For example,

---

37   Benjamin Alarie and Richard M. Bird, "Canada", in G. Bizioli and C. Sacchetto (edits), *Tax Aspects of Fiscal Federalism: A Comparative Analysis*, International Bureau of Fiscal Documentation, Amsterdam, 2011, p.82.

38   Robin Boadway and Anwar Shah, *op. cit.*, p.171.

while VAT is under the jurisdiction of the national government in Nigeria, its administration and revenues are shared with the states.[39] In Australia, while VAT/Goods and Services Tax (GST) is administered by the national tax administration, all revenue is distributed to the sub-national governments (States and Territory).[40] In Canada, attempts have also been made to coordinate provincial sales tax with the national GST and the former tax is now being levied in the name of harmonised sales tax in Nova Scotia, New Brunswick, Ontario, Newfoundland & Labrador, British Columbia and Nova Scotia on the same base as of the national GST and is administered together with the GST by the national tax administration.[41]

There are, however, a few exceptions. For example, while several attempts were made to levy VAT at the national level in India, a consensus could not be reached between the federal and the state governments. Hence, VAT is independently levied by the states, and preparations are underway for the introduction of a national level VAT, which means VAT will be levied both by the national and the state governments side by side on the same base. In Canada, while Quebec levies an independent VAT in addition to national VAT, three provinces i.e. Prince Edward Island, Manitoba and Saskatchewan, still levy a separate sales tax at the retail level, which is in addition to the national level GST.[42]

While it is appropriate to levy VAT at the national level from different points of view, upper level sub-national governments should have access to this important source of revenue. It indicates the need to levy VAT as a shared tax, where VAT is administered by the national government but the revenue is shared between the national and sub-national governments.

Excise duties:

Excise duties are also considered better members of the national tax family and are basically levied by the national governments in various countries, including federal Australia and Nigeria. If these duties are levied at the sub-national level, with different rates in different tax

---

39   For more reasons why a sub-national VAT is infeasible or undesirable see Richard M. Bird, "Local and Regional Revenues: Realities and Prospects," in Richard M. Bird and Francois Vaillancourt (edits.), The World Bank, Washington DC, 2006 p.187; and Roy Bahl, *Intergovernmental Transfers in Developing and Transition Countries: Principles and Practice*, Municipal Finance, Background Series 2, The World Bank, April 2000, p.10.

40   Cost of collection of the national tax administration is deducted from the GST collection before it is distributed to the sub-national governments.

41   Benjamin Alarie and Richard M. Bird, *op. cit.*, p.121.

42   Benjamin Alarie and Richard M. Bird, *op. cit.*, pp.121-122.

jurisdictions, they may promote distortions in the economy and encourage cross border shopping problems, particularly in the case of light goods such as cigarettes that are easy to transport. Besides, as excise duties are also levied to achieve broader social objectives, which is basically a national level function, they need to be levied by the national government. As excise duties are levied to supplement VAT, a national tax, these duties are further justified to be levied at the national level on items where it is difficult to levy VAT or with different rates, to inject progressivity in the commodity tax system. Like VAT, excise duties should be levied by the national government, but the excise revenue may be shared between the national and sub-national governments.

Income taxes:

Income taxes are levied on the income of individuals or businesses. While a tax levied on the income of individuals is known as PIT, a tax levied on the income of businesses is known as BPT. As these taxes are levied for both stabilisation and distribution purposes, they are considered better members of the national tax family. Furthermore, as income taxes are more sensitive to economic conditions and are less stable, they are not suited at the sub-national level. Besides, BPT has other special reasons to be levied at the national level which are as follows:

- BPT can be collected efficiently and cost-effectively only at the national level because of the nature of its base. This tax is levied by the national government on the profit earned by a legal entity through its nationwide operation and is collected from its Headquarters. It would be complicated to collect this tax by the sub-national governments on the branches/subdivisions of a legal entity that are located under their jurisdictions. If it is collected from the legal entity on the basis of its registration or location of the head office, it would not be fair since the tax revenue will be received only by the sub-national government where the legal entity is registered or its headquarters is located and other sub-national governments where the branches/subdivisions of the legal entities are located would be deprived of BPT revenue.

- The BPT base is less evenly distributed than the tax base of many other taxes.[43] In many countries big companies located under the jurisdictions of a few sub-national governments provide a large tax base. Imposition of BPT at the sub-national level would only increase horizontal fiscal disparities amongst the sub-national governments.

---

43   Jorge Martinez-Vazquez, Andrey Timofeev, and Jameson Boex, *op. cit.*, p.105.

- The burden of the BPT may be exported outside the jurisdiction of sub-national government, when it is levied at the sub-national level. This tends to undermine "political accountability and responsible local governance."
- The BPT base is less stable than even the base of the PIT. So the BPT is not appropriate at the sub-national level.

Because of the abovementioned reasons, income taxes are assigned to the national government in different federal countries including Australia, Germany and Nigeria. There are, however, practices to levy some kind of income tax at the sub-national level in some countries, including Canada and the USA where, as discussed later, sub-national level income taxes are collected basically in the form of piggy-backing on the national income taxes. In India, state governments are authorised to levy income tax on agricultural income.

On administrative grounds, PIT is relatively easier to levy at the sub-national level as the burden of this tax is basically borne by the local residents. "In most developing and transition countries, the individual income tax is essentially a payroll tax, with capital income and earnings of the self-employed generally outside the tax base. This makes the calculation of income tax entitlements to a particular province an easier matter than in the case of the VAT or the corporate income tax."[44]

Natural resource taxes:

Natural resource taxes are generally considered as national level taxes as their base is distributed highly unequally between jurisdictions and if they are levied at the sub-national level, they lead to horizontal fiscal imbalance. On the other hand, these taxes may be considered appropriate at the sub-national level in some way from efficiency point of view as they are levied on resource endowments that are immovable across jurisdiction, their administrative cost would not be excessive and "the taxation of resources goes hand in hand with their management, which is more efficiently done at the state level."[45] That is why in some countries such as Canada they are managed by the state governments. In other countries, sub-national governments are given a portion of revenue collected from natural resource tax, where the base of natural resource tax is located. For example, in South Sudan, of the net oil and other mineral revenues, two percent is provided to producing state and three percent to the local bodies of that area. In general, "one might opt for maintaining federal control of those resources which are more

---

44   Roy Bahl (2000), op. cit., pp.10-11.
45   Robin Boadway and Anwar Shah, *op. cit.*, pp.186-187.

likely to be important and unequally distributed, such as oil and gas and mining, while decentralising others that are less important, such as quarrying and perhaps forestry."[46]

Stamp duties:
While stamp duties can be levied both at the national and sub-national levels, the common international practice under the federal system is to levy this tax at the state level. For example, stamp duties are levied by the state governments in Australia, and the USA.

Registration fees:
Registration fees are levied on the transfer of ownership of property such as land and vehicles. These fees should be assigned to that level of government that has authority to maintain land records and vehicle registration.

Property taxes:
Property based taxes satisfy most of the principles of local taxation, including autonomy, accountability, localisation of tax base and non-exportability as follows:

- The principle of autonomy advocates that local governments should have adequate fiscal autonomy in order to raise sufficient revenues to enable them to respond to the needs and preferences of the people within the jurisdiction.[47] Local governments should have the authority to adjust some aspects of local taxes, such as tax rates, in accordance with local conditions. Property taxes satisfy the principle of autonomy since a variation in the rates or bases of these taxes are likely to cause fewer distortions in the economy than would similar variations in income and commodity taxes, i.e. resources are not likely to be diverted due to differentiation in property taxes unless the base and rate differentiation is sufficiently large among local governments.

- The principle of accountability advocates that local tax system should promote the accountability of the local government. For this to occur, the electorate should be aware of the tax liability and is therefore expected to maintain an interest in expenditure patterns of local governments and thus is expected to voice any perceived abuse by the local authority. Property taxes provide a high degree of accountability due to their visibility.

---

46   *Ibid.*, p.187.
47   The absence of fiscal autonomy of local governments would not enable their development
       as autonomous bodies.

- The base of property tax is localised and less mobile between jurisdictions. It is "usually clear which local government is entitled to tax a particular property. A local profit tax, for example, lacks this advantage."[48]

- As property taxes are cyclically stable, they contribute towards a stable source of revenue for the local tax system as fluctuations in revenue and dependence on central governments for income can potentially weaken local governments.

Entertainment tax:

Entertainment tax is also considered an appropriate local tax. Local governments are better equipped to monitor entertainment establishments and thus ensure the effective implementation of this tax.

User charges:

"Wherever possible, charge" should be the first rule of local finance as charges levied on the direct recipients of benefits are considered efficient.[49] They are also appropriate at the higher levels.

As per the principles and international common practices, all major taxes such as VAT, excise duties, customs duties, and income taxes are levied at the national level while property taxes and entertainment taxes and registration fees are collected at the sub-national level in the EAC countries. For example, while the national government can levy taxes through the enactment of a law as per Article 152 of the Ugandan Constitution, Article 191 authorises the local governments to levy rents, rates, royalties, stamp duties, personal graduated tax, cess, fees on registration and licensing and any other fees and taxes that Parliament may prescribe. In Rwanda, while national government levies all the major taxes such as customs duties, VAT, excise duties, and income taxes, local governments collect property tax, trading license and rental income tax. Similar situations exist in other East African countries such as Kenya and Tanzania.

---

48   *Ibid.* p.17.
49   Richard M. Bird, *op. cit.*, p.212.

Taxes assigned to/levied by national and sub-national government in East African countries are summarised in the following table:

Table 7.5: Taxes Assigned to/Levied by Different Levels of Governments in the EAC Countries

Country	Tiers of Government	Tax Authority
Burundi	National	Customs duties, VAT, excise duties, PIT, BPT
	Local	Vehicle tax, real estate tax
Kenya	National	Customs duties, value-added tax, excise tax, income tax, user charges and any other tax or duty, except property tax or entertainment tax that it is authorised to impose by an Act of Parliament, user charges
	Local	Property rates, entertainment taxes, user charges and any other tax that it is authorised to impose by an Act of Parliament
Rwanda	National	Customs duties, VAT, excise duties, PIT, BPT
	Local	Property tax, rental income tax, and trading licenses
Tanzania	National	Customs duties, VAT, excise duties, income tax payable by individuals and by corporations
	Local	Development levy, head tax, property tax, service levy, business license fee on trade, crop and livestock cess, other fees and user charges
Uganda	National	Customs duties, VAT, excise duties, PIT, BPT.
	Local	Rents, rates, royalties, stamp duties, cess, fees on registration and licensing and any other fees and taxes that Parliament may prescribe (property taxes, license and user charges)

7.5 Methods of revenue generation at sub-national level

According to subsidiarity in taxation, a given tax should be assigned to the lowest level of government that can implement it.[50] Fiscal decentralisation advocates the control of sub-national governments over their own taxes in-terms of tax bases, rates, and administration. Tax assignment rules provide guidance for the assignment of a given tax at the sub-national level. A given tax again can be collected in

---

50   Charles E. McLure and Jorge Martinez-Vazquez, *op. cit.*, p.14.

different ways such as an independent tax, nationally administered tax, piggybacking or a shared tax as follows[51]:

7.5.1 Independent taxes

Sub-national taxes can be levied as independent taxes, which are controlled fully by the sub-national governments, i.e., sub-national governments determine their bases, fix their rates, administer them and retain revenue collected from these taxes. Independent taxes promote autonomy since sub-national governments can adjust the structure of these taxes as per local needs. As these taxes are fully controlled by the sub-national governments, they are accountable for the successes or failures of these taxes as "accountability would probably be greater if taxpayers had to grapple directly with a provincial tax office."[52] Besides, it is possible to bring all small businesses under the tax net as local governments are aware of the economic activities taking place in their jurisdiction. There is also a continuous flow of revenue to the local government coffer from the implementation of independent taxes. Independent taxes, however, are costly to the tax administration as each sub-national tax administration has to be involved in the collection of its own tax. But it may lack qualified staff and is deprived of the economy of scale which takes place under a nationally administered system. It is also costly to the taxpayers to comply with two separate national and sub-national taxes, which are administered by two different tax administrations. It is even more so in the case of businesses that have operation in the jurisdictions of different sub-national governments as they have to follow different procedures relating to different taxes levied by different sub-national governments. Different structures of independent taxes levied by various sub-national governments also invite distortions as resources are likely to be diverted from one tax jurisdiction to another in response to tax.

7.5.2 Nationally administered taxes

Sub-national taxes can also be administered by the national tax administration, though their bases and rates are controlled by the sub-national governments. For example, in Canada, national tax administration administers the provincial PIT surcharge for all provinces

---

51   Pros and cons of different methods may be found in Roy Kelly, "Intergovernmental Revenue Allocation Theory and Practice: Application to Nepal," Development Discussion Paper No. 624, Harvard Institute for International Development, Harvard University, February 1998.

52   Benjamin Alarie and Richard M. Bird, *op. cit.*, p.113.

except for Quebec and BPT for all provinces except for Alberta and Quebec.[53] Similarly, as stated earlier, the national tax administration administers the harmonised sales tax of most of the provinces in Canada. Lower level government's tax administration, however, can assist the national tax administration in providing information about the tax base which is otherwise difficult for the national tax administration to obtain.

National tax administration of sub-national taxes provides different advantages, including economy of scale and application of uniform procedures throughout the country. This is economical for the local tax administration and taxpayers. It, however, "can affect the behaviour of tax officials, who may concentrate their efforts on collecting central government taxes at the expense of those allocated to sub-national jurisdictions."[54] There may also appear the problem of mutual mistrust among the levels of governments.

7.5.3 Piggy-backing

Sub-national taxes also can be levied in the form of piggy-backing. This can be done in two ways:

- Sub-national government can fix surcharge on the tax base assigned by the national tax legislation i.e. tax-on-income.
- Sub-national government can levy surcharge on the national tax amount, as determined by the national tax law, i.e. tax-on-tax.

Under either case, sub-national governments do not have control over the tax base, which is fixed by national government. Sub-national governments, however, have power to fix the rate of surcharge within or without the limit fixed by the national government. This means that it satisfies the principle of autonomy to some extent as sub-national governments can adjust tax rates according to the local conditions. As sub-national governments fix the tax rates, it makes them accountable since local constituents would raise voice if the tax paid by them is mismanaged. But it is also possible that "states may indulge in unstable competition by reducing the tax rates to attract investments or divert trade in their favour. Such a competition resulting in 'the race to the bottom' only results in the states losing revenue and creating distortions in resource allocation."[55] It indicates the need to fix the minimum and

---

53   *Ibid*, p.111.

54   Jorge Martinez-Vazquez, Andrey Timofeev, and Jameson Boex, *op. cit.*, p.119.

55   M. Govinda Rao and Tapas K. Sen, "Federalism and Fiscal Reform in India," Working Paper No. 2011-84, National Institute of Public Finance and Policy, New Delhi, February 2011, p.11.

maximum limits beyond which sub-national governments cannot levy the surcharge rate to check unfair competition amongst the sub-national governments.

Surcharge is administratively simple for both local tax administration and taxpayers. Sub-national tax administrations do not have to put efforts to collect it and taxpayers do not have to comply with two different taxes, do not have to study two different laws or follow provisions relating to two different taxes and make separate calculations for two different taxes.[56] There is no need to submit separate returns for sub-national surcharge and pay this tax separately. Surcharge is included in the national tax returns, and paid together with the national tax. National tax administration collects the surcharge and remits it to the local governments. This results in low compliance cost. However, "there is substantial risk that the higher level government collecting the revenues will not remit them to the sub-national government."[57] Such a possibility can be avoided by adopting a system where the taxpayers may be required to deposit surcharge amount directly to the account of the sub-national government. Besides, national tax administrators may not be keen in implementing sub-national surcharges effectively. There might be mistrust between the national and sub-national tax administrations. It would be necessary to set-up a joint committee of national and sub-national governments to monitor the collection and distribution process of sub-national surcharge and avoid/minimise mistrust between the two tax authorities.

Now the question is, which taxes can be collected as piggy-backing at the sub-national level? As stated earlier, customs duties, BPT, and VAT are basically national taxes and are also not suitable to be collected by the sub-national governments as piggy-backing on national taxes. Customs duties are levied on imports and exports, so there is no question of levying this tax by sub-national government in any form. No examples can be found of sub-national piggy-backing on the national customs duties around the world. BPT is levied on the profit of a legal entity and is collected from its headquarters. This means it will not be easy to levy BPT as a surcharge on national BPT by each sub-national government where the subdivisions of a legal entity are located. VAT is also basically

---

56   There are, however, some exceptions. For example, in Switzerland, as cantons have authority to determine levels of exemptions or deductions, taxpayers are required to make separate calculations for the canton and federation taxes that might lead to variations in the taxable income of the cantons and the confederation.

57   Charles E. McLure and Jorge Martinez-Vazquez, *op. cit.*, p.13.

a national tax. Due to the more stable tax base, one could argue that VAT can be levied by a higher level sub-national government as a surcharge on the national VAT; but it is difficult to apportion VAT as "credits and liabilities for the tax arise in different jurisdictions and there is no simple way to attribute the tax on a derivation basis unless an explicit, and arbitrary, formula is used."[58] Besides, it would bring distortions if levied with different rates by different sub-national governments.

It is possible to levy sub-national piggy-backing on national PIT at a flat rate to be fixed by the sub-national governments and revenue could be given on a resident or place of work basis.[59] For example, sub-national governments levy piggybacking on the national PIT in Canada and the USA. Sub-national governments also could levy surcharge on the national excise duties as is done in Canada and the USA.

7.5.4 Shared taxes

Some taxes can be shared by the national and sub-national governments. Rates of shared taxes are set by the national government, which also assesses and collects the tax.[60] Revenue from the shared tax can be distributed on a derivation basis, i.e. revenue provided to local government as a share of a tax that is collected within their boundaries. Alternatively, the revenue can be distributed between the national and sub-national government on the basis of some formulae. As sub-national governments do not have power to control base and rates of shared taxes, they do not provide autonomy to the sub-national governments which cannot adjust the structure of the shared taxes as per the local needs. Besides, national tax administration may not be interested in implementing shared taxes effectively when the large part of the shared tax collection goes to the sub-national governments. There is also a risk that the national government collecting the revenues from the shared taxes may not remit them to the sub-national government[61] fully or partially in a timely manner.

Which tax is common to be used as shared tax? PIT is considered to be more appropriate to be levied as a shared tax. BPT is not suitable since it is difficult to find the tax collected within the area of sub-national

---

58   Jorge Martinez-Vazquez, Andrey Timofeev, and Jameson Boex, *op. cit.*, p.133.
59   While the distribution of surcharge on the national PIT on a place of work basis is easier from an administrative point of view as the tax withheld by an employer is remitted to the sub-national government where the employer is located, resident basis is justified since an employee's large share of consumption of public services is believed to take place in the area where he resides.
60   Richard M. Bird, op. cit., p.213.
61   Charles E. McLure and Jorge Martinez-Vazquez, op. cit., p.13.

governments. In practice, VAT is levied as a shared tax in some countries which is distributed on the basis of some formulas. For instance, in Germany VAT is levied as a shared tax where tax legislation is federal and tax base and rates are controlled by the federal government, tax administration is state (*länder*) and revenue is divided among federal, state and local governments. Of the total VAT revenue, the federation receives 9.5% for old age pensions and the unemployment fund. The remaining amount is split up as following: The municipalities receive 2.2% in compensation for the elimination of the capital business tax; the rest is divided between the federation and the states (*länders*) at a 50.5:49.5 ratio.[62] The amounts for the three levels are not allocated in the form of derivation-based sharing. Instead, they receive their amounts from the total collected fund, i.e. more like transfers. In Nigeria also, VAT is levied as shared tax where the national government controls tax rates and base, collects it and revenue is shared between the national, state and local governments at rates fixed from time to time.

In Australia, while excise duties are federal, federal government cannot use more than one fourth of the excise revenue and the balance needs to be paid to the states, or applied towards the payment of interest on debts of the states taken over by the federal government.

In Kenya 5% of national PIT is given to the local authorities. In Tanzania fuel levy revenue is divided on a 70%:30% ratio to the national and sub-national governments. In Rwanda, revenue generated from the tax on rental income is transferred by the national government to the local governments.

---

62   Arthur B. Gunlicks, "German Federalism: Theory and Developments, German Federalism and Recent Reform Efforts," German Law Journal, 06 No. 10, 2005, p.1284.

7.7.5 Shared revenue

Under the shared revenue system, the entire pool of national tax revenue can be shared with the sub-national government. Revenue is collected by the national government and fully or partially shared with sub-national governments on the basis of a formula that takes into account the origin of revenues, population, tax capacity, or revenue need. For example, in Kenya revenue raised nationally shall be shared equitably among the national and county governments. Here at least 15% of the entire pool of national revenue is distributed to the sub-national governments.

7.6. Fiscal imbalance

As stated earlier, on both efficiency and equity grounds, all modern major taxes vis., VAT, excise duties, customs duties, and income tax are better collected at the national level. On the other hand, many services can be provided efficiently at the local level. Furthermore, there are significant differences among the local governments in terms of revenue generation and service delivery capacity. This means that there is a mismatch between expenditure and revenue between the levels of government and among the sub-national governments, leading to both vertical and horizontal imbalance.

Vertical Imbalance:

As stated above, most buoyant taxes are more efficiently and equitably collected at the national level, while many of the more costly services are administered better at the sub-national level. Accordingly, there is a worldwide tendency to assign almost all major taxes to the national governments and many expenditure responsibilities are given to sub-national governments. The need for the local governments providing such services as social service and water supply increases further with economic growth and urbanisation.[63] There is thus a mismatch between functions and finance between different levels of government in various countries that leads to 'vertical imbalance'.

EAC countries also face the problems of vertical fiscal imbalance as the sub-national governments are assigned more expenditure responsibilities than can be financed from their own sources of revenue. For example, total local government expenditure in Uganda in 2007/08 was UGX 975.9 million against total own source revenue of UGX 146.7 million, indicating a huge fiscal gap between the income and expenditure

---

63   Roy Bahl (2000), *op. cit.*, p.1.

of local governments.[64] Similarly, in Tanzania, while local governments collect roughly 5% of all public revenues, they are responsible for about 20% of public spending.

Horizontal Imbalance:
Sub-national governments generally differ regarding resource capacity and needs. For example, the tax base is generally concentrated in the capital cities and other urban areas where most of the industry and trade take place. On the other hand, expenditure responsibilities may be high in the rural areas where there is lack of modern amenities but very limited revenue base. Expenditure responsibilities also may vary between sub-national governments depending upon demographic situation. For example, local bodies with a high share of children and old people may have higher education and health expenditure requirements than those of other areas. Similarly, expenditure requirements are also affected by geographical location. All these factors result in horizontal imbalance.

Thus there is an imbalance between revenues and expenditures of sub-national governments in different countries, including the EAC countries. The gap between the expenditure and revenue of the sub-national governments can be closed by means of various methods, including revenue sharing, grants and borrowings.

7.7. Inter-governmental transfer

Inter-governmental transfers commonly refer to funding received from other levels of government, generally by the lower level governments from the higher level governments. They are provided to achieve different objectives including the following:[65]

- Improve vertical and horizontal fiscal balance.
- Compensate for the presence of spill-overs or externalities between jurisdictions in the provision of public services at the sub-national level.
- Fund "merit goods."

Inter-governmental transfers may take place in the form of revenue-sharing and grants. As revenue sharing has already been discussed earlier in this section we will concentrate on grants from national to

---

64   CLFG, Country Profile: Uganda, the Local Government System in Uganda, p.234. See: www.clfg.org.uk.
65   The United Republic of Tanzania President's Office, *op. cit.*, p.92.

sub-national governments that constitute a large portion of the inter-governmental transfers. While grants may take different forms, they are divided into four categories for the purpose of the current chapter:

- Unconditional grants
- Conditional grants
- Equalisation grants
- Other grants (such as matching grants, cost reimbursement (full or partial) grants, donor grants, etc.)

7.7.1 Unconditional grants

Unconditional grants, also known as block grants or general grants are defined as the transfer of money from the higher level government to the lower level government without any conditions. They can be used by the receiving government in ways as per their requirements. As they come with no strings in terms of minimum standards of service delivery or any performance indicators, they may be used at the discretion of sub-national government to provide services in line with the local demand. In this sense they provide more autonomy to the sub-national governments in utilising the grants as per local needs. Unconditional grants "are typically the appropriate vehicle for purposes of fiscal equalisation. The purpose of these grants is to channel funds from relatively wealthy jurisdictions to poorer ones. Such transfers are often based on an equalisation formula that measures the "fiscal need" and "fiscal capacity" of each province, state, or locality."[66]

Unconditional grants are commonly used in the EAC countries. For example, the Ugandan Constitution defines unconditional grants as the minimum grants that are paid to local governments to provide decentralised services. The amount of unconditional grants is calculated annually on the basis of a formula which includes the unconditional grant of the previous year, corrected by the increase in the general price level, plus the net change in the budgeted costs of running newly devolved or subtracted services.[67] Thus the provision of unconditional grants in Uganda reflects the "devolution of functions and its budgetary implication" as they are calculated annually with reference to the reassignment of tasks between the national and sub-national

---

66   Wallace E. Oates, *op. cit.*, p.1127.
67   Article 13 Schedule 7 of the Ugandan Constitution.

governments. As indicated in Table 7.6, in 2007/08, local governments in Uganda received UGX 131.3 million in unconditional grants from the national government which was 15.13% of total grants, 12.94% of total income (own source revenue and transfers) and 13.45% of total expenditure in that year.

Table 7.6: Aggregate Revenue and Expenditure for Local Governments in Uganda in 2007/08

Income	Amount (000,000)	Expenses	Amount (000,000)
Local Revenues	146.7	Administration	122.9
Local Taxes	79.0	Finance	51.2
Property Income	67.7	Statutory bodies	35.9
Transfers	867.8	Production	50.3
Unconditional grants	131.3	Health	120.8
Equalisation grants	3.5	Education	448.0
Conditional transfers	733.0	Works	97.8
		Natural resources	3.9
		Community services	18.8
		Planning unit	214.4
		Internal audit	24.8
Grand Total	1014.5	Grand total	975.9

Source: CLFG, Country Profile: Uganda, The Local Government System in Uganda, p.234. www.clfg.org.uk.

7.7.2 Conditional grants

Conditional grants are defined as transfer of money from the higher level government to the lower level for specific purposes that may not be used for any other purpose. These grants come with strings where conditions are tied to the use of the grants or to the performance to be achieved through the use of the fund. Thus some restrictions are placed on the use of conditional grants. As per the agreements completed with the national governments, these grants need to be used to carry out some specified services such as primary healthcare, primary education, etc. and are required to meet minimum standards. They are also provided to carry out local services that generate benefits for residents of other jurisdictions.[68] As these grants come with strings, they cannot be used by local government freely as per local requirements. More strings mean lesser autonomy for sub-national governments in using the grants, thereby undermining the role of decentralisation.

Conditional grants are commonly seen in the EAC region also. The Ugandan Constitution defines conditional grants as "monies paid to local governments to finance programs agreed upon between the central government and the local governments and expended for the purposes for which they are made and in accordance with the conditions agreed upon." Conditional grants constitute a large part of the total grants received by the local governments from the central government. For example, in Uganda, as given in Table 7.6, local governments received UGX 733 million conditional grants from the national government in 2007/08 which was 84.47% of total grants, 72.25% of total income (own source revenue and transfers) and 75.11% of total expenditure in that year.

7.7.3 Equalisation grants

As stated earlier, sub-national governments differ in terms of revenue potential as well as geographical condition, demographic situation and level of development. This leads to variation in the revenue generating capacity and expenditure requirements across the sub-national governments, which are corrected by equalization grants. They are provided to those sub-national governments whose tax base is smaller than average but expenditure needs are above the average. For example, in Denmark "[m]unicipalities with tax base above average and expenditure needs below average pay some money into an equalization fund. This money is then redistributed to those municipalities with tax bases below average and expenditure needs above average."[69] In Canada, it is a "constitutionally mandated unconditional block transfer designed to support reasonably comparable levels of services at reasonable levels of taxation. The program uses a national average standard as the basis for equalization."[70] While equalisation grants are provided to smooth out differences in tax bases and expenditure needs amongst the sub-national governments, they might encourage sub-national governments to understate their tax bases to attract higher grants from the national government.

---

68   Wallace E. Oates, *op. cit.*, p.1127.
69   Republic of Uganda, Local Government Finance Commission, *op. cit.*, p.14.
70   *Ibid*, p.14.

Equalisation grants play a major role in many countries, including Australia, Canada, and Germany, where there are substantial transfers of income from wealthy provinces or states to poorer ones.[71] Equalisation grants are used in the EAC countries also. For example, the Ugandan Constitution defines the equalisation grant as "…the money to be paid to local governments for giving subsidies or making special provisions for the least developed districts; and shall be based on the degree to which a local government is lagging behind the national average standard for a particular service." As indicated in Table 7.6, equalisation grants constitute only a small part of the total grants in Uganda. In Kenya there is established an Equalisation Fund into which shall be paid one half per cent of all the revenue collected by the national government each year. The national government shall use the Equalisation Fund only to provide basic services including water, roads, health facilities and electricity to marginalised areas to the extent necessary to bring the quality of those services in those areas to the level generally enjoyed by the rest of the nation, so far as possible. The national government may use the Equalisation Fund:

- only to the extent that the expenditure of those funds has been approved in an Appropriation Bill enacted by Parliament; and

- directly, or indirectly through conditional grants to counties in which marginalised communities exist.

7.7.4 Other grants

Other grants may include matching grants, cost reimbursement grants, donor provided grants, etc. Matching grants are provided by the national government to the sub-national governments as co-funding to carry out certain activities at the sub-national level. They encourage sub-national governments to generate more revenue, which, however, aggravates problems of horizontal imbalance. Sub-national governments also receive funds in the form of cost reimbursement grants, which may be full or partial reimbursement of funds used to carry-out certain activities. Sub-national governments sometimes receive grants also from donors other than the higher levels of governments.

---

71   Wallace E. Oates, *op. cit.*, p.1127.

7.8 Borrowing

There may be a gap between the expenditure and revenue/grants of the national and sub-national governments, which can be closed by borrowings. While such a situation is expected to arise during times of financial crises, wars, natural calamities etc. it has become common to borrow money by various levels of government in different countries.

Governments may borrow money through the issuance of various kinds of debt instruments including bonds or securities. Individuals as well as organisations buy these debt instruments that, on maturity, are paid with principal and interest as per the contract. Governments may borrow money internally as well as externally. External loans can be raised through the sale of debt instruments to foreign governments, organisations and so on, while internal loans can be mobilised through the sale of debt instruments to citizens and organisations within the country.

In the EAC region also both national and sub-national governments are authorised to borrow money to carry out their functions. For example, in Kenya both the national and local governments can borrow. Parliament may, by legislation, prescribe the terms on which the national government may borrow. Similarly, a county government may borrow only if the national government guarantees the loan and with the approval of the county government's assembly. Parliament shall prescribe terms and conditions under which the national government may guarantee loans.

In Uganda, national government may borrow from any source. Government, however, shall not borrow, guarantee, or raise a loan on behalf of itself or any other public institution, authority or person except as authorised by or under an Act of Parliament. Similarly, local governments, with the approval of national government, may borrow money to carry out their functions.

It is important to establish prudent/strict rules relating to the borrowing by various levels of governments. For example, in Germany local governments can use borrowing only for investment purpose, borrowing should be used only when other financing is not feasible or appropriate and borrowings should be taken only with the approval of regional governments.[72] Tough rules were introduced in 2001 in

---

72   Fabrizio Balassone, Daniele Franco, and Stefania Zotteri, "Fiscal Rules for Sub-national Governments, What Lessons from EMU Countries?," A Paper prepared for the Conference on "Rules-Based Macroeconomic Policies in Emerging Market Economies"

sub-national government finances in Sweden where sub-national governments were required to balance their budget every year and, when a deficit was recorded, the balance had to be restored within two years.[73]

7.9. Institutional set-up

National level fiscal matters are, in general, managed by the national Ministry of Finance. Similarly, state level fiscal matters are generally dealt with by the State Ministry of Finance under a federal system. Besides, line ministries of the national governments are responsible for overseeing overall matters relating to sub-national governments. For example, the Uganda Ministry of Local Government, Kenya Ministry of Local Government, Tanzania Ministry for Regional Administration and Local Government,[74] and the Rwanda Ministry of Local Government, Good Governance, Community Development and Social Affairs oversee the matter of sub-national governments in the respective countries.

There is also a common practice to constitute an independent commission to handle fiscal matters in different countries including EAC countries.

---

jointly organised by the IMF and the World Bank, Oaxaca Mexico, February 14-16 2002, May 2002, p.25.

73   Fabrizio Balassone, Daniele Franco, and Stefania Zotteri, *op. cit.* p.13.

74   In Tanzania, different central government ministries and agencies handle different aspects of the local government finance system. For example, the Minister of Finance (MoF) is broadly responsible for coordinating inter-governmental fiscal relations, the Prime Minister's Office – Regional Administration and Local Government (PMO-RALG) ensures proper local financial management through the issuance of local budget guidelines, procedures, and instructions on the development of the local budget, as well as through the provision of technical support and capacity building. It also monitors local expenditures and revenue collections and audits local government budgets to assure that local budgets are implemented or executed as planned. There is an inter-ministerial Local Government Finance Working Group represented by MoF, PMO-RALG, Ministry of Planning and Economic Empowerment (MPEE), the President's Office - Public Service Management (PO-PSM), as well as key line ministries.

Examples are: Joint Finance Commission in Tanzania, Local Government Finance Commission in Uganda[75] and Commission on Revenue Allocation in Kenya. Major responsibilities of these bodies are stated below:

Table 7.7: Responsibilities of Local Finance Bodies in the EAC

Country	Organisation	Responsibilities
Kenya	Commission on Revenue Allocation	The Commission is responsible for: 1. making recommendations concerning the basis for the equitable sharing of revenue raised by the national government: between the national and county governments; and among the county governments. 2. making recommendations on other matters concerning the financing of, and financial management by, county governments, as required by the constitution and national legislation.
Tanzania	Joint Finance Commission	The functions of the Commission are: to analyse the revenue and expenditure arising from, or relating to the management of affairs concerning Union Matters, and to make recommendations to the two Governments concerning the contribution by, and the allocation to each of the Governments. to keep under constant scrutiny the fiscal system of the United Republic and also the relations between the two Governments in relation to financial matters. to discharge other functions which the President shall assign to the Commission or as the President may direct, and in accordance with a law enacted by Parliament.

---

75   In Uganda the Commission undertook studies to examine whether imbalance existed between service delivery assignments on the one hand and revenue generation possibilities of local governments, on the other.

Country	Organisation	Responsibilities
Uganda	Local Government Finance Commission	Main functions of the Commission include: advise the President on all matters concerning the distribution of revenue between the Government and Local Governments and the allocation to each Local Government of money out of the consolidated fund. consider in consultation with the National Planning Authority and recommend to the President the amount to be allocated as equalisation and conditional grants and their allocation to each Local Government. consider and recommend to the President potential sources of revenue for Local Governments. advise the Local Governments on appropriate tax levels to be levied by Local Governments. mediate in case a financial dispute arises between Local Governments and advise the Minister accordingly. analyse the annual budgets of Local Governments to establish compliance with the legal requirements and notify the Councils concerned and the President through the Minister for appropriate action. recommend to the President through the Minister, the percentage of the National Budget to be transferred to Local Governments every financial Year. recommend to the President, Central Government taxes that can be collected by Local Governments in their respective jurisdiction on an agency basis. perform such other functions as may be prescribed by law.

Similarly, many more stakeholders, including different line ministries, constitutional or non-constitutional committees, and associations of sub-national governments are involved in one way or the other in the inter-governmental fiscal relations issues. Some countries have created high level political forums to handle intergovernmental fiscal relations issues. For example the Council of Australian Governments oversees federal-state financial arrangements and coordination of regulation, service delivery and harmonisation reform in Australia.[76] It is critical, particularly for the success of a federal system to maintain close cooperation between different levels of government, resolve sticky fiscal issues formally/informally and harmonise tax and other fiscal matters vertically and horizontally.

7.10 Summary

Inter-governmental fiscal relationships reflect the respective assignment of expenditure and revenue responsibilities between the national and sub-national governments. While some responsibilities are exclusively carried out by one level of government, such as national defence and foreign affairs by the national government, and garbage collection and street cleaning by the local governments, others may be carried out by different levels of government though on different scale. In case of many responsibilities, while there are no hard and fast rules regarding which ones should be assigned to which level of government, services providing benefits only to the local constituents should be at the lowest level of government, state/provincial government should provide those services when benefits accrue to more than one local government jurisdiction, and national government should provide those services when benefits accrue to the whole nation.

On the revenue front, while taxes suitable for economic stabilisation, progressive re-distributional taxes and tax bases distributed highly unequally between jurisdictions should be assigned to the national government and taxes that have bases with low mobility between jurisdictions and cyclically stable taxes should be assigned to the sub-national governments. On the other hand, both the national and sub-national governments may be given authority to levy benefit taxes and user charges.

---

76   Miranda Stewart, Chapter 4 Australia, in Benjamin Alarie and Richard M. Bird, "Canada", in G. Bizioli and C. Sacchetto (edits), *Tax Aspects of Fiscal Federalism, A Comparative Analysis*, International Bureau of Fiscal Documentation, Amsterdam, 2011, p.121.

Sub-national taxes can be collected in the form of independent taxes, nationally administered taxes, piggy-backing and shared taxes. Revenue collected from the shared taxes can be distributed on a derivation basis, meaning that each jurisdiction gets the same share of the revenue collected in its area. Alternatively, the revenue can be distributed between the national and sub-national government on the basis of some formulae. Sub-national governments can also get financial resources from the national government in the form of grants. Both the national and sub-national governments can also borrow money to finance deficits.

As elsewhere, in the EAC region, various levels of government have authority to generate their own sources of revenue and decide how to use their revenue to provide public services. As these countries have been implementing decentralisation programs, they have been transferring more and more expenditure responsibilities to the sub-national governments. As the local governments know the requirements of their constituents better than the national governments, they can tailor programs to match the demand of their constituency. This is expected to enhance efficiency. However, tax assignments in these countries seem inappropriate as major revenue sources are not only limited to the national level, they have not been developed as shared taxes. As a result, there is a huge gap between demand and supply of fiscal resources at the sub-national level, which has been met mainly by inter-governmental transfers that cover almost 90% of all local government spending, while local governments' own source revenues and local government borrowings account for a nominal share of local financial resources. This indicates the need to reform inter-governmental fiscal relations in the EAC region.

Appendix 7a: Distribution of Functions between the National and County Governments in Kenya

National Government	County Government
1. Foreign affairs, foreign policy and international trade	1. Agriculture, including (a) crop and animal husbandry; (b) livestock sale yards; (c) county abattoirs; (d) plant and animal disease control; and (e) fisheries
2. The use of international water resources	2. County health services, including, in particular (a) county health facilities and pharmacies; (b) ambulance services; (c) promotion of primary health care; (d) licensing and control of undertakings that sell food to the public; (e) veterinary services (excluding regulation of the profession); (f) cemeteries, funeral parlours and crematoria; and (g) refuse removal, refuse dumps and solid waste disposal
3. Immigration and citizenship	3. Control of air pollution, noise pollution, other public nuisances and outdoor advertising
4. The relationship between religion and state	4. Cultural activities, public entertainment and public amenities, including (a) betting, casinos and other forms of gambling; (b) racing; (c) liquor licensing; (d) cinemas; (e) video shows and hiring; (f) libraries; (g) museums; (h) sports and cultural activities and facilities; and (i) county parks, beaches and recreation facilities
5. Language policy and the promotion of official and local languages	5. County transport, including (a) county roads; (b) street lighting; (c) traffic and parking; (d) public road transport; and (e) ferries and harbours, excluding the regulation of international and national shipping and matters related thereto.
6. National defence and the use of the national defence services	6. Animal control and welfare, including (a) licensing of dogs; and (b) facilities for the accommodation, care and burial of animals
7. Police services, including (a) the setting of standards of recruitment, training of police and use of police services; (b) criminal law; and (c) correctional services	
8. Courts	
9. National economic policy and planning	
10. Monetary policy, currency, banking (including central banking), the incorporation and regulation of banking, insurance and financial corporations	
11. National statistics and data on population, the economy and society generally	
12. Intellectual property rights	
13. Labour standards	

National Government	County Government
14. Consumer protection, including standards for social security and professional pension plans	6. Animal control and welfare, including (a) licensing of dogs; and (b) facilities for the accommodation, care and burial of animals
15. Education policy, standards, curricula, examinations and the granting of university charters	7. Trade development and regulation, including (a) markets; (b) trade licenses (excluding regulation of professions); (c) fair trading practices; (d) local tourism; and (e) cooperative societies
16. Universities, tertiary educational institutions and other institutions of research and higher learning and primary schools, special education, secondary schools and special education institutions	8. County planning and development, including (a) statistics; (b) land survey and mapping; (c) boundaries and fencing; (d) housing; and (e) electricity and gas reticulation and energy regulation
17. Promotion of sports and sports education	9. Pre-primary education, village polytechnics, home craft centres and childcare facilities
18. Transport and communications, including, in particular (a) road traffic; (b) the construction and operation of national trunk roads; (c) standards for the construction and maintenance of other roads by counties; (d) railways; (e) pipelines; (f) marine navigation; (g) civil aviation; (h) space travel; (i) postal services; (j) telecommunications; and (k) radio and television broadcasting	10. Implementation of specific national government policies on natural resources and environmental conservation, including (a) soil and water conservation; and (b) forestry
	11. County public works and services, including (a) storm water management systems in built-up areas; and (b) water and sanitation services
	12. Firefighting services and disaster management
	13. Control of drugs and pornography
	14. Ensuring and coordinating the participation of communities and locations in governance at the local level and assisting communities and locations to develop the administrative capacity for the effective exercise of the functions and powers and participation in governance at the local level

17. Promotion of sports and sports education

18. Transport and communications, including, in particular (a) road traffic; (b) the construction and operation of national trunk roads; (c) standards for the construction and maintenance of other roads by counties; (d) railways; (e) pipelines; (f) marine navigation; (g) civil aviation; (h) space travel; (i) postal services; (j) telecommunications; and (k) radio and television broadcasting

National Government	County Government
19. National public works	
20. Housing policy	
21. General principles of land planning and the co-ordination of planning by the counties	
22. Protection of the environment and natural resources with a view to establishing a durable and sustainable system of development, including, in particular (a) fishing; hunting and gathering; (b) protection of animals and wildlife; (c) water protection, securing sufficient residual water, hydraulic engineering and the safety of dams; and (d) energy policy	
23. National referral health facilities	
24. Disaster management	
25. Ancient and historical monuments of national	
26. National elections	
28. Health policy	
29. Agricultural policy	
30. Veterinary policy	
31. Energy policy including electricity and gas reticulation and energy regulation	
32. Capacity building and technical assistance to the counties	
33. Public investment	
34. National betting, casinos and other forms of gambling	
35. Tourism policy and development	

Chapter 8

Tax Administration

8.1 Semi-Autonomous Revenue Authorities (SARAs)

All the EAC Partner States have created SARAs to implement their national tax policies. This approach was initiated in the region by Uganda, which set up the Uganda Revenue Authority (URA) on 5 September 1991. While Kenya created the Kenya Revenue Authority (KRA) on 1 July 1995, Tanzania established the Tanzania Revenue Authority (TRA) on 1 July 1996. Rwanda Revenue Authority (RRA) was adopted in 1997 and Burundi Revenue Authority (BRA) became operational in 2010.

In the EAC region, SARAs have been created by Special Acts,[1] and exist outside the civil service in place of the different revenue departments that were formerly part of the civil service. For example, while KRA replaced the Customs and Excise Department, the Income Tax Department and the VAT Department,[2] URA replaced the Customs

---

1   See the following acts: Uganda Revenue Authority Act 1991, Kenya Revenue Authority Act 1995, Tanzania Revenue Authority Act 1995 and Burundi Revenue Authority Law 2009. While RRA was initially set up under Law no. 15/97 of 1997, it is currently governed by Law No. 08/2009 of 27 April 2009 on Determining the Organization, Functioning and Responsibilities of the Rwanda Revenue Authority.

2   Sec. 23 Kenya Revenue Authority Act 1995.

Department, the Income Tax Department and the Inland Revenue Department.[3]

SARAs have been created to provide more autonomy to the tax administration in terms of human and financial resources.[4] The tax administration must have an environment supportive to the development of efficient, energetic, experienced and honest professionals, who are by far the most important factors in determining its efficiency. The tax administration must have the power to hire, fire, reward and motivate its staff. This is more likely to happen under a SARA, than under a government department due to the rigid civil service rules. The experience shows that "SARAs generally are able to provide better pay and other incentives to their staff while also imposing greater accountability for performance."[5] This has encouraged EAC countries to take their tax administrations out of the civil service and place them under SARAs. This has provided greater flexibility in establishing conditions of service in order to retain existing competent staff and attract promising new staff. The SARA should also have autonomy in spending its budget according to the needs of the tax administration. In general, SARAs all over the world are designed, as Taliercio (2004) observes, "with a number of autonomy-enhancing features, including self-financing mechanisms, boards of directors with high ranking public and private sector representatives and *sui generic* personnel system."[6]

SARAs are corporate bodies working as government agencies under the general supervision of the Finance Minister. They are responsible for assessing and collecting taxes, customs duties and for a few specified non-tax revenue sources, such as motor vehicle fees. RRA also has initiated the collection of social contributions from July

---

3   Sec. 19 Uganda Revenue Authority Act 1991.

4   For example, the reasons for creating the TRA were twofold: "first to eliminate the direct political influence of the Ministry of Finance on the day-to-day operations of the tax administration. And second, to raise the salary of tax officials without parallel increases for the rest of the public sector." See O.-H. Fjeldstand, "Fighting Fiscal Corruption: The Case of the Tanzania Revenue Authority," Chr. Michelson Institute Development Studies and Human Rights, Working Paper 2002:3, p.10.

5   M. Gallagher, Benchmarking Tax System, Public Administration and Development, 2005, p.9, available at http://frp2.org/english/Portals/0/Library/Tax%20Administration/ Benchmarking%20Tax%20Systems%20-%20Full%20Text.pdf.

6   R. Taliercio Jr., "Designing Performance: The Semi-Autonomous Revenue Authority Model in Africa and Latin America," World Bank Policy Research Working Paper 3423, October 2004, p.2.

2010.[7] SARAs also advise the Finance Ministers on tax policy and administration and on the revenue implications of new tax measures.

While SARAs are overseen by a board in each country in the EAC region, the number of board members and their appointment varies from country to country.[8] In Tanzania, the total membership of the board, including the Chairperson, is ten. The Chairperson and the Commissioner General are appointed by the President, four members are appointed by the Finance Minister and the remaining four are ex-officio members.[9] The total number of board members is seven in Rwanda and Uganda, but the composition of the board is different in these two east African nations. In Rwanda, six members of the board are appointed by an order of the Prime Minister and the Commissioner General is appointed by a Presidential Order. In Uganda, the board consists of the Chairperson, two other members and the Commissioner General appointed by the Finance Minister, and representatives of the Ministry of Finance, Ministry of Trade and Industry, and Uganda Manufacturers Association. Kenya has the largest board in the region with 11 members consisting of a Chairperson appointed by the President, four members and the Commissioner General of KRA appointed by the Finance Minister. The remaining members are ex-officio members.[10]

The Chairperson of the board of directors is appointed by the President in Kenya and Tanzania, by the Prime Minister in Rwanda and by the Finance Minister in Uganda. The Commissioner General of the RRA is appointed by the President in Rwanda and Tanzania, and by the Finance Minister in Kenya and Uganda. In order to strengthen autonomy, experts believe that "the chairperson of the board of directors should be appointed by the President, approved by the legislature, and subject to a fixed term of service."[11]

SARA boards have representation from various sectors as there are some ex-officio members from specified government offices,

7   African Development Bank Group, *Domestic Resource Mobilization for Poverty Reduction in East Africa: Rwanda Case Study*, November 2010, p.14.
8   Board members, other than ex-officio members, are appointed for three years and eligible for re-appointment only for a period not exceeding three years in Kenya, Rwanda, Tanzania and Uganda.
9   Permanent Secretary of the Ministry of Finance of the Union Government, Principal Secretary of the Ministry of Finance of the Zanzibar Government, Governor of the Bank of Tanzania and Permanent Secretary of the Ministry of Planning.
10   Permanent Secretary of the Ministry of Finance, Permanent Secretary of the Ministry of Commerce and Industry, Finance Secretary of the Ministry of Finance, the Attorney-General or its representative, and the Governor of the Central Bank of Kenya.
11   R. Taliercio, *op. cit.*, p.52.

representatives from the private sector and some appointed members who are expected to be experienced in financial, commercial, tax or legal matters. In order to promote the autonomy of a SARA, experts consider that the public sector representatives on the board of directors should serve in an ex-officio (i.e. a non-voting) capacity.[12] Regarding the appointment of the private sector members, Mann (2005) suggests that private sector candidates for board membership may be recommended by an independent advisory committee[13] instead of being appointed by the Finance Minister or appointed as ex-officio members. This might enhance the possibility of recommending an expert who could work without fear of reprisal.

Appointing members from the private sector may attract a broader talent pool that might yield an approach that is more oriented toward customer service. It also helps to reduce corruption and negative political influence. On the other hand, there is a possibility of conflicts of interest and breach of taxpayer confidentiality by the private sector members.[14]

It is also important not to make the size of the board too large since it would make it difficult to schedule meetings, to reach a consensus and to make members more accountable. A too small board size may not be able to provide sufficient support or may not have the desired experience among its members to carry out its responsibilities. Jenkins (1994) considers the number of members should be between five and nine.[15]

SARAs are funded in different ways in the EAC countries. For example, a certain percentage of the collected revenue is given to the SARAs in Kenya[16] and Rwanda.[17] In Uganda, while parliament established the budget for the SARA, the Finance Minister can authorise the URA to retain a percentage of the revenue collected by the URA in order to enable it to meet its expenditure without interruption, which, however,

---

12   *Ibid.* p.52.
13   Arthur J. Mann, Are Semi-Autonomous Revenue Authorities The Answer To Tax Administration Problems In Developing Countries? – A Practical Guide, Fiscal Reform in Support of Trade Liberalization Project, 2004, p. 5, available at http://pdf.usaid.gov/pdf_docs/Pnadc978.pdf.
14   G. Jenkins & R. Khadka, Modernization of Tax Administration in Low-Income Countries: The Case of Nepal, CAER II Discussion Paper 68, Harvard Institute for International Development (HIID), September 2000, p. 30.
15   Glenn P. Jenkins, Modernization of Tax Administrations: Revenue Board and Privatization as Instruments for Changes, 1994, p. 78, available at www.queensjdiexec.org/publications/qed_dp_113.pdf.
16   Funding is limited to 2% of revenue collections. See: sec. 16 KRA Act.
17   RRA can retain a maximum of 3.5% of revenue collected.

should not exceed the amount of approved budget.[18] In Burundi and Tanzania's SARAs, the budget is appropriated through parliament. Taliercio (2004) observes that "a percentage-based mechanism coupled with automatic retention of funds would not only insulate the SARA from the pernicious effects of a weak PEM (public expenditure management) system but could also provide hard incentives to increase collections."[19]

The annual accounts of SARAs are audited by the Auditor General in Uganda, where the Commissioner General is required to submit an annual report to the Finance Minister who, in turn, submits it to the Parliament. KRA's Commissioner General is also required to submit an annual report to the Finance Minister and its accounts are audited by the Controller and Auditor General. The SARAs publish annual reports, including audited financial reports, prepare strategic plans and are accountable to the parliament.

The experiences of the EAC and other countries implementing SARAs indicate that while the creation of SARAs provides a platform from which the change can be facilitated, their mere establishment offers no guarantee of success. Their performance depends on "the strength and quality of SARA leadership, political will and sustained public and private sector support."[20] Furthermore, a detailed preparation does not only play a big role in the smooth transition to a SARA but also in its overall success. In this context, the issues of degree of autonomy, the governance framework, financing mechanism, human resources, accountability and scope of the SARA in terms of the revenue sources to be collected by a SARA need to be examined carefully and appropriate decisions need to be taken.

---

18   Sec. 14 Uganda Revenue Authority Act 1991.
19   . R. Taliercio, *op. cit.*, p.8.
20   A. Mann, *op. cit.*, p.3.

Besides, if the international experience of implementing SARAs is any indication, countries contemplating the introduction of a SARA will have to consider the following aspects very seriously in order to implement the SARA in a meaningful manner:[21]

- formation of a steering committee;
- development of a concept paper regarding the appropriate structure, governance, staffing, financing mechanism, autonomy and accountability of a SARA;
- preparation of draft legislation and its passage by the parliament;
- design of an organisational structure and staffing;
- assessment of office space, equipment and budget;
- change management strategy;
- appointment of board and commissioner general;
- transfer/hire staff; and
- training/seminars for staff.

8.2. Unified

EAC SARAs are created as unified administrations in place of various fragmented independent revenue departments.[22] This means all tax administration is put under the one umbrella of a SARA. As there are many similarities in the administration of various taxes, there is a trend around the world to unify different tax administrations.[23] Such a unified tax administration possesses several advantages over the fragmented tax administrations.

Unified tax administration is advantageous for both taxpayers and tax collectors. As taxpayers have to visit only one tax office for all taxes, this reduces their burden and compliance costs. They can receive better services at a lower cost. On the other hand, as tax officials have to deal with each taxpayer only once for all the various taxes, it saves tax administration time. The time saved by tax officers can be spent on other

---

21   For details, see B. Crandall & M. Kidd, *A Toolkit For Implementing A Revenue Authority (RA)*, Caribbean Regional Technical Assistance Center, International Monetary Fund, November 2009, pp.15-28.

22   Under a fragmented system, different revenue departments are created to deal with different types of taxes or different groups of taxes. Under any of these systems, taxpayers have to visit many different tax offices
and various tax officials have to deal with the same taxpayers. This leads to higher collection and compliance costs. There is also a lack of co-operation among various revenue departments, they do not share information relating to taxpayers, and there is no uniformity in the procedures relating to the settlement of different taxes.

23   For example, Canada, Denmark and the United Kingdom.

activities. This means that unified administration helps government to collect tax revenue at a relatively lower cost.

Unified tax administration also improves coordination between different units. For example, it is much easier to coordinate the activities of the customs and tax administration when they are part of one management rather than two separate bodies. Customs information is important to determine income tax or VAT liability. Similarly, information collected for income tax or VAT may be useful for customs administration. In addition, flow of information between customs and domestic taxes is much easier under a unified administration than two separate independent organisations. Besides, a unified system enables the tax administration to maintain overall effective control over taxpayers. With such a system in place, the tax administration would know the different taxes each taxpayer should pay, the payments he has or has not made, and the fines or arrears, if any, on his account. Integration of various tax bodies enables "maximum synergies from more in-depth information on taxpayers while facilitating tax payments through a single window, consolidation of data availability through a common data warehouse, and the conduct of analysis to support tax policy and administrative policymaking."[24]

There are also advantages from the information technology point of view. For example, it is much easier to define an information technology strategy for one unit than it is to define one across different independent organisations, which requires very close co-ordination (which is often lacking). It is much cheaper to install and maintain a computer system in one unit than running it in parallel in different organisations. Similarly, harmonising the procedures relating to various taxes is much better for both the taxpayers and tax administration, which is again easier in one unit than in different independent organisations. Unified organisation also provides advantages of economies of scale and makes it easier to establish a single database.

---

24   P. Shome, *Tax Shastra, Administrative Reforms in India, United Kingdom and Brazil*, BS
Books, 2012, p.162.

8.3 Mixed structure

The organisational structure of SARAs in the EAC does not strictly follow a particular pattern (such as tax type[25] or function[26] or taxpayer segments[27]) and can best be termed as a "mixed structure." For example, the TRA is divided into different units which are created by type of tax (such as Commissioner for Domestic Revenue and Commissioner for Customs and Excise), by major tax functions (such as Commissioner for Tax Investigation and Director for Taxpayer Service and Education) and by taxpayer segments (such as the Commissioner for Large Taxpayers and the Commissioner of Domestic Revenue, which administers small and medium taxpayers). Similarly, the URA consists of departments which are created by type of tax (such as Domestic Taxes Department and Customs Departments) and by function (such as Corporate Services Department and Tax Investigation Department). Similarly, the RRA has two distinct operational departments: Customs and Excise Department and Domestic Taxes Department. There is also a practice of dividing the Domestic Taxes Department into a large taxpayer office and a small and medium taxpayer office. In addition, all EAC SARAs have different support function departments, such as human resources and administration department, finance department, planning and research department, information technology department, and legal services and board affairs department. EAC SARAs also have an internal audit department.

It is common in the EAC countries to create separate departments for customs and tax within a single SARA, which has a unified management and which shares corporate resources. There is some rationale for keeping tax and customs departments separate. As Gill (2003) observes, "Even though the revenue collection processes are broadly similar in tax and customs administration, customs functions relating to regulation of trade flows, prevention of prohibited goods and anti-smuggling are significantly different and require maintenance of specialized skills within the merged organization."[28]

---

25   Under the organisational structure based on type of tax, different departments are created to administer different taxes separately (for example, income tax department, excise department, sales tax department, property tax department and customs department).
26   Under the functional structure, tax organisations are divided into different units by major tax functions, such as taxpayer service, registration, return processing, refund, audit and collection.
27   For example: large taxpayer office, medium taxpayer office and small taxpayer office.
28   J.B.S. Gill, "The Nuts and Bolts of Revenue Administration Reform," Lead Public Sector Management Specialist Europe and Central Asia Region, 2003, p.10 available at http://

While there is no consensus regarding a single best form of organisational structure and it is common to maintain customs and tax as two separate departments along with the common support function departments, it is desirable to organise customs and tax departments on functional lines. For example, the tax department may be divided into different units to take care of each major tax function (vis., taxpayer service, registration, return processing and revenue accounting, refund, collection and audit). Similarly, the customs department may be divided into different functional sections, such as tariff and classification, valuation, PCA, bonded warehouse/duty drawback, exemption and border control.

In the same way, tax and customs field offices may also be structured on functional lines. For example, tax offices may have taxpayer service, registration, return processing, revenue accounting, refund, collection and audit sections, whereas customs offices may have valuation, PCA, bonded warehouse, duty draw back and exemption and border control sections. Both tax and customs offices may have support function sections, which may have different units, depending upon the size and requirements of an office.

The advantages of a functional-based organisation are:

- specialisation in tax administration;
- economies of scale;
- one window for taxpayer inquiries;
- common registration functions;
- single accounting framework;
- collection and audit across taxes;
- integrated information processing operations;
- effective implementation of all tax functions; and
- improved management and control in tax administration.

8. 4 Taxpayer segment focus

8.4.1. Introductory remarks

All taxpayers are not equally important for the tax administration from a revenue point of view, nor are their tax obligations similar. Small taxpayers who may have to pay only one or two types of taxes need a simplified scheme for the payment of their tax liability. Medium-sized taxpayers should also have simple filing and payment requirements. In contrast, large taxpayers need to follow standard book-keeping, invoicing, filing and payment procedures. That is why there has been a practice of combining functional focus with the taxpayer focus and creating separate offices for small, medium-sized and large taxpayers.

8.4.2. Large taxpayer office

EAC countries have created large taxpayer offices (LTOs) within the tax administration to cater to large taxpayers who provide the bulk of the tax revenue in a way that best suits their needs.

Commonly cited advantages of the creation of a separate LTO are:

- faster and easier services to large taxpayers;
- effective control of large taxpayers;
- protection of a large amount of revenue; and
- increase in the level of voluntary compliance of large taxpayers.

Large taxpayers are generally identified on the basis of annual turnover. There is also the practice of identifying large taxpayers on the basis of the economic nature of a business. For example, in some countries businesses such as banks, insurance companies, telecommunication companies or oil companies are treated as large taxpayers without any further qualification. Some EAC countries have also included the amount of the paid/payable tax in the list of selection criteria for large taxpayers.

In the EAC region, Kenya initiated an LTO in 1998 to provide one-stop-shop services to large taxpayers. It was created as a fully-fledged office in 2006,[29] which is largely structured on functional lines as follows:

- taxpayer service;
- compliance and debt management, including return processing; and
- audit.

Kenya identifies large taxpayers on the basis of the following criteria:[30]

- all companies with an annual turnover over KES 750 million and their subsidiaries and associates;
- banks and insurance companies;
- oil exploration companies;

---

29   See http://www.kra.go.ke/index.php/large-taxpayers-office/about-lto/vision.
30   *Ibid.*

- all tobacco companies;
- manufacturers of wines and spirits, subject to turnover threshold;
- state corporations with annual turnover/budget over KES 750 million;
- head office operations of central government ministries and departments of local authorities with City status; and
- top 200 VAT payers and 30 excise duty payers.

This office administers about 400 large taxpayers, which provide about 75% of domestic tax revenue.[31]

While Uganda initiated an LTO in the URA in 1998, it was totally revamped as a fully-fledged LTO in February 2005.[32] It is largely structured on functional lines with a taxpayer service section, return, and payment and enforcement section, refund section, system and procedures section together with two sectoral sections: Financial and Manufacturing Section and Service, General Trade Government and Oil Section.

Large taxpayers are identified in Uganda on the basis of the following criteria:

- annual turnover above UGX 5 billion;
- domestic tax revenue above UGX 2 billion;
- banks, holding companies and their associates; and
- excise duties paying firms.

The LTO in Uganda administers about 500 large taxpayers who provide about 70% of domestic tax revenue.

In Tanzania, a large taxpayer department was initially created within the TRA on 1 October 2001, and was later converted into a fully-fledged department in 2003.[33] It is divided into four sections: audit, data processing and examination of returns, debt management and technical services.

Originally, large taxpayers in Tanzania were identified on the basis of the following two criteria:

- nature of sectors, such as financial institutions and mining companies; and
- annual total tax payment of over TZS 400 million for three consecutive years.

---

31   *Ibid.*
32   The Commonwealth Association of Tax Administrators, "Implementing Large Taxpayer Units," 2006, pp.43-46, available at www.catatax.org/upiloads/051006/LTU.report.20.4.06. pdf.
33   *Ibid.*

- Later on taxpayers with over TZS 10 billion turnover were also included in the large taxpayer list.

While the LTO initially started the administration of about 100 large taxpayers, it currently administers about 400 taxpayers, which provide over two thirds of total domestic tax revenue.

In Rwanda, an LTO was created as one of the two offices (the other office is the small and medium taxpayers' office) under the Domestic Tax Department, which was created in April 2006.[34]

Large taxpayers in Rwanda are identified on the basis of the following criteria:

- complex activities and annual turnover over RWF 200 million;

- required to pay excise duties;

- registered with Rwanda Development Board and have invested over RWF 300 million; and

- gauged to have growth potential and their annual PAYE costs exceed RWF 600 million.

There are over 300 large taxpayers, which account for over 50% of the total RRA tax revenue.

Any country contemplating the development of an LTO will have to carefully examine various options as follows:

> First, the large taxpayer office can be created in the tax headquarters to carry out audit of the large taxpayers as was initially done in some countries, including Nepal. In such a case, this unit will deal only with the tax audit of large taxpayers. As the bulk of the tax revenue comes from a few large taxpayers who pay high taxes, audit of these taxpayers needs to be carried out on the basis of risk assessment in an effective manner by qualified staff expected to maintain better control over large taxpayers and to ensure better service and uniform treatment. There are, however, some limitations with this type of structure. For example, since the LTO will conduct tax audits and other tax offices will perform all other functions, including the collection of officially assessed tax as a result of the tax audit, there may be a lack of coordination between the tax offices and the large taxpayer audit unit. Besides, since the LTO only conducts tax audits, there may be a lack of effective supervision of all the functions related to large taxpayers. For example, there may be lack of a swift and efficient service to large taxpayers and lack of sufficient efforts towards increasing the level of voluntary tax compliance on the part of taxpayers.

---

34   African Development Bank Group, *op. cit.*, p.24.

Second, the LTO can be developed as a fully-fledged office, which should be responsible for all the tax administration functions relating to large taxpayers in order to make the services swift, efficient and available at a central point as is done in many countries. Some countries (such as Nepal), which initially set up an LTO with only an audit function, have later made these offices responsible for all tax functions relating to large taxpayers. As stated above, LTOs have been developed as fully-fledged offices in the EAC region.

Either way, the bottom line is that there will be a need for the administration of large taxpayers by qualified efficient staff who have knowledge of accounting, auditing and tax laws. Tax offices usually lack qualified staff that could be expected to handle larger taxpayers in the desired way. Besides, large taxpayers are not located in one area; their branches and businesses are spread all over the country. This means that one local tax office cannot have a close view of the total transactions of a large taxpayer. A unit of the headquarters or a separate fully-fledged office created to deal only with large taxpayers is likely to have more qualified staff that can be expected to maintain better control over large taxpayers and also to ensure better service and uniform treatment. There are also economies of scale, and the possibility of maintaining standards and uniformity through the operation of an LTO.

In order to develop an LTO as a fully-fledged office, it is necessary to design the structure of the office along functional lines, ensuring that there are adequate physical facilities available, and to develop specific requirements in terms of qualification, training and experience for prospective employees. The idea should be to develop this office as a model for implementing reform measures in the tax administration – the experience gained at an LTO could be replicated elsewhere in the subsequent phases of reform.

Arguably, this office could have control over a larger chunk of the revenue and taxpayers, provided it could ensure swift and effective service to large taxpayers, which would in turn lead to greater compliance among large taxpayers. However, due precaution must be taken before setting up the office. Detailed preparation concerning manpower, monitoring mechanisms, budget and physical facilities has to be in place before the creation of such an office. There could be a higher risk of corruption if it is created just as "one more office" without taking into consideration a number of factors that contribute towards abuse of authority.

8.4.3. Small and medium tax office

There has been a practice in the EAC countries to establish a separate office to administer small and medium-sized taxpayers. For example, in Rwanda, a small and medium-sized tax office was created in April 2006 within the Domestic Tax Department.[35] In Tanzania and Uganda, small and medium-sized taxpayers are dealt with by the Domestic Revenue Departments of TRA and URA, respectively. Kenya has gone one step further by establishing a separate medium taxpayer office on 1 November 2010 to deal with medium-sized businesses with turnovers ranging from KES 300 million to KES 750 million.[36]

The objectives of the medium taxpayer office were:
- to enhance high voluntary tax compliance;
- to ensure better service delivery through taxpayer segmentation based on the taxpayers' industry;
- to entrench relationship management that caters for taxpayers' need on a personal basis;
- to ensure professionalism and integrity of tax administration;
- to carry out focused quality audits based on an objective risk profiling framework; and
- to foster close working relationships with taxpayers through industry association and tax professionals.

The medium tax office is structured on functional lines as follows:
- taxpayer service (customer care, registry, online service support, taxpayer education and refunds);
- compliance and debt (relationship management, debt collection, queries and disputes, return processing and enforcement); and
- audit (procedural audits, refund claims audit, objections and appeals).

8.5. Responsibilities of the headquarters

8.5.1. Introductory remarks

There are variations in the organisational structure of EAC SARAs, which have created many departments by tax functions, broad tax categories and taxpayer segment. In order to make things simple, the next sections consider that a SARA has three departments: tax department, customs department, and support function department at headquarters, and tax and customs offices are structured on functional lines.

---

35   *Ibid.*
36   See http://www.kra.go.ke/index.php/domestic-taxes/medium-taxpayers-office.

8.5.2. Tax department

The tax department is mainly responsible for enforcing various taxes under its authority. It develops policy, plans and programs, outlines operational guidelines, designs forms and instruction manuals, and monitors and evaluates their implementation by field tax offices. Typical responsibilities of the various sections of a tax department are as follows.

Taxpayers' *service section* develops tax education materials, such as brochures, FAQs, pamphlets, posters and videos. It organises television and radio programs, and tax information sessions/seminars for taxpayers. It maintains public relations and a help desk to assist and educate taxpayers on various aspects of taxation. It also responds to taxpayers' queries and distributes tax information materials to them.

The taxpayer service function is crucial for raising the level of voluntary tax compliance among the taxpayers and for the implementation of the self-assessment system in a proper manner. These are the most important aspects of modern tax administration. Under the self-assessment system, taxpayers are required to assess their tax liability, report it and pay the tax due in a timely manner. For this to happen to the extent desired, it is necessary to enhance the understanding of the tax system among the taxpayers by means of tax education and provision of taxpayer assistance. The bottom line is that taxpayer service should be provided to a larger section of the taxpaying population.

The *registration section* is concerned with outlining strategy relating to registration, de-registration, defining the requirements for registration, outlining registration application procedures and procedures relating to the issuance of registration certificates and taxpayer identification numbers (TINs). It is also responsible for suggesting methods of operation when taxpayers move from one tax office's jurisdiction to another and for developing procedures relating to cancellation of registration. It also designs forms and manuals used for registration/de-registration of taxpayers.

Proper registration and issuance of TINs is basic to any tax administration. This determines the success of other tax functions, such as return and payment processing, audit and collection. Every attempt must be made to register all potential taxpayers and to issue one TIN to one taxpayer, ensuring that each taxpayer should be issued only one TIN. The registration database should be updated regularly and should not contain any bogus or non-existent taxpayers.

The *return processing and revenue account section* develops policy and procedures relating to filing, payment and maintenance of taxpayers' accounts. It processes tax returns and maintains taxpayer's individual accounts. It also prepares various management information system (MIS) reports and provides periodic reports to the management and other sections of the tax department.

The return and payment processing function is critical for maintaining a taxpayer master file and for processing returns and payments in a timely manner. It is necessary to simplify return and payment processing requirements, asking taxpayers to submit only necessary data and documents, and to gradually develop electronic filing systems. There should be a system to ensure that every penny paid by a taxpayer is deposited in his account in a timely and correct manner. There should also be a system to reconcile data between the tax administration, treasury and banks. Effective registration, proper issuance of TIN, and timely and accurate processing of returns and payments facilitate the collection and audit work.

The *refund section* deals with refunds to the taxpayers as well as diplomatic missions and foreign-funded projects, which may benefit tax refunds under international protocols. It also draws up refund verification procedures.

The *audit section* is responsible for developing an audit policy, plan/program and related strategy. It defines different levels of audits, selection criteria for audits and selects taxpayers for audit. It also draws up procedures, develops instructions, forms and manuals for audit. It also monitors and evaluates the audit activities of the field tax offices.

The role of the audit section is critical under a modern tax administration. Taxes, in general, are assessed and paid by taxpayers under the self-assessment system. Tax audit is crucial to make taxpayers cautious in assessing their tax liability correctly and paying it in a timely manner. It must be remembered, however, that the tax administration does not have enough resources to audit every taxpayer. It may not be cost effective to chase small taxpayers. A proper tax audit/compliance improvement strategy which ranges from less intrusive to more intrusive treatments, depending on the type of risk needs to be adopted. This approach would make an audit program cost effective.

While collection measures are important, it must be remembered that the tax administration does not have enough resources to collect every amount owed. It may not even be cost effective to try to collect small amounts, so a proper tax collection strategy is required. Targets should be fixed in terms of the amount to be collected, number of tax arrears cases to be closed and the percentage of arrears to be reduced to a certain level. It is necessary to identify recent and undisputed arrears of high amounts where the possibility of collection is high, to give high priority to recent and undisputed arrears of high amounts, to prepare records by age and amount, tax type and industry, and to authorise tax officials to write off arrears which are not collectible up to certain amounts.

8.5.3. Customs department

The Customs Department is mainly responsible for enforcing customs duties, VAT and excise duty on imports. It is involved in outlining operational guidelines, program development, evaluation, and designing forms and instruction manuals. Typical major sections of the various sections of the Customs Department are as follows:

- Tariff and classification section deals with the classification of goods. It provides advice to importers and exporters on the classification;
- Valuation section deals with valuations of goods and develops guidelines relating to customs valuation;
- Exemption section deals with the duty exemption provided to diplomats and foreign-aided projects;
- PCA section develops strategy, procedures and guidelines regarding PCA. PCA is an audit based control which is intended to verify the accuracy and authenticity of the traders' declarations, commercial data and accounts after the goods have been taken out of customs custody;
- Bonded warehouse/duty drawback section deals with the goods imported under the bonded warehouse system and handles the duty drawback mechanism;
- Trade facilitation section deals with the overall customs policy that facilitates legitimate trade and ensures timely clearance of goods and facilitates speedy movement of travellers;
- Border patrol section develops strategy and policy in order to maintain border control (together with security and other organisations). It establishes techniques and methods to combat smuggling or illegal trade; and
- Customs agents section deals with the licensing and registration of customs agents and other related issues.

8.5.4. Support function department

The support function department is responsible for carrying out functions other than core tax and customs functions. It may have the following sections to deal with several support functions:

- personnel and general administration section (responsible for personnel management, staffing and overseeing physical facilities);
- financial administration section;
- training section (responsible for developing and conducting trainings);
- legal section (responsible for provision of legal advice to the management of the SARA, tax and customs offices);
- appeal section (responsible for administrative review);
- information technology section;
- statistics, research and analysis section (responsible for forecasting revenue, estimating revenue impact of tax proposals, collecting revenue and other relevant fiscal/economic data and preparing periodic reports on revenue and functional activities);
- international relations section (responsible for international tax matters, tax treaties, international and regional trade and customs organisations, such as the EAC, WTO and World Customs Organization);
- file management section;
- investigation section (responsible for monitoring market cycles, conducting a follow-up on whether or not invoices are issued in the desired way, penalising those who do not issue invoices the way they should, conducting unannounced audits and investigating cases of fraud and smuggling); and
- internal audit section (responsible for reviewing the performance of the tax and customs administration).

8.6. Field office responsibilities

8.6.1. Tax office

The tax office is responsible for the implementation of the tax system. Typical sections of the tax office include the following:

- taxpayers service section which provides assistance to taxpayers, educates them on various tax issues, prepares and distributes taxpayer education materials, provides taxpayers with forms, conducts preliminary checks of submitted forms and delivers notices to taxpayers;
- registration section which receives completed registration application forms from the taxpayer service section, verifies taxpayer's physical address, assigns TINs, issues registration certificates to taxpayers, takes

necessary action to trace and register potential taxpayers, maintains a taxpayer registration database and carries out deregistration;

- return processing and revenue account section which processes returns and maintains accounts of taxpayers;

- refund section which processes refund claims, conducts refund verification visits, approves/recommends the payment of refunds and writes reports on refunds.

- audit section which is involved in the preparation, conduct and reporting of desk and field audits;

- collection section which deals with tax arrears, maintains a follow-up record of those who have not yet filed their tax returns, those who have filed late and those who have arrears against their account. It obtains the non-payers list from the return processing and revenue account section, prioritises arrears by amount, age, and likelihood of collection success, and initiates tax arrears collection activities in a most cost effective way; and

- support function sections which may include: administration section, finance section, IT section, legal section, and file management section to carry out support activities at the tax offices.

8.6.2. Customs office

Customs offices are responsible for assessing and collecting customs duties, preventing fraud and smuggling, and controlling carriers, persons and articles entering into and leaving the country. These offices are also involved in collecting VAT and excise duties on imports. Major functions of the various sections of the customs office are as follows:

- tariff and classification section which applies appropriate tariffs to the imported and exported goods and provides advice to the importers/ customs agents on the classification of commodities and applicable customs rates;

- valuation section which is involved in the valuation of imported/exported goods for the application of customs duties and taxes;

- revenue section which collects revenue on imports and exports, including excise duties and VAT;

- PCA section which carries out post-clearance audit at the trader's premises after goods have been released from customs' custody to verify the accuracy and authenticity of the traders' declarations and traders' commercial data and accounts;

- bonded warehouse/duty drawback section which deals with the goods imported under the bonded warehouse system and handles duty drawback matters; and border patrol.

8.7. Voluntary tax compliance

The EAC countries have adopted a self-assessment system where taxpayers are required to assess their tax liability, submit their tax returns and pay up the tax due. Taxpayers' accounts and returns are accepted at face value, unless tax officials find discrepancies during the course of a tax audit. The success of such a self-assessment system depends, among other things, on the level of voluntary compliance of the taxpayers. That is why raising the level of voluntary tax compliance is considered as one of the important functions of a modern tax administration. Voluntary compliance could be raised through a set of the following promotional and regulatory measures.

The tax system should be made simple. It is necessary to implement a few broad-based taxes instead of numerous independent taxes and to make their structures simple by limiting the number of tax rates and special provisions. Tax procedures need to be made simple and transparent, and taxpayers may be asked to submit only such information and documents as are likely to be useful and which are otherwise unavailable.

Taxpayers should be educated about their rights and responsibilities through tax brochures, pamphlets, posters, tax seminars, television and radio programs, newspaper articles and advertisements. The increasing trend to establish taxpayer call centres makes it possible to provide required information to taxpayers over the phone, thereby avoiding the need for physical contact between the taxpayers and tax officials. Taxpayers should be reminded regularly about the deadlines for submission of tax returns and payment of tax.

The tax administration must have procedures in place for those who opt not to comply and ensure that taxpayers are aware of those procedures. Continuous follow up should be conducted, so that those who do not voluntarily participate in the tax system are warned about their non-compliance, those who do not submit returns are reminded about it, appropriate actions are taken against those who do not pay tax in time, and audit and investigation activities are carried out in order to minimise the scope for tax evasion. The tax administration also has to penalise those who break the rules. This can be shown by the compliance model (see Diagram 8.1).

Diagram 8.1: Compliance Model

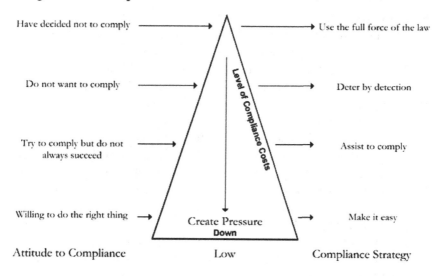

Source: Inland Revenue, Annual Report 2001-2002, Part 2- Overview of 2001/02, New Zealand, p.19.

Most of the taxpayers at the bottom line want to pay tax, but need a simplified system. Second grade taxpayers want to comply but may not always succeed. Tax officials should assist them to comply by way of tax education and assistance. Some taxpayers do not want to comply, so that some immediate action for compliance is necessary. This can be done by conducting a survey of potential taxpayers and informing them that they must register, sending reminders to non-filers and asking non-payers to pay. Financially tough measures are needed for a small group of taxpayers who decide not to comply, so that the bottom line taxpayers can feel satisfaction with their regular compliance.

8.8 Strategic planning

EAC SARAs have been adopting three- to five-year strategic plans[37] that contain their vision, mission and values, together with strategic goals, objectives, actions, resources and time frame.[38]

The process was first initiated in the region by Uganda in the mid-1990s, when it adopted its first five-year strategic plan for the period 1995/96-1999/2000. It "had not been fully internalized and the necessary staff were therefore not assigned to this function. Planning was top-down, leading to lack of support by staff."[39] The URA's second strategic plan for 2002/03-2006/07 was designed on the basis of the bottom-up consultative process,[40] which was launched on 24 October 2002. "The Plan's focal point is to maximize central government tax revenue and also improve the corporate image of the organization. Its vision is for URA to ultimately collect revenue that will fully finance government's recurrent and development expenditure."[41] Uganda implemented its third strategic plan for the period 2006-2010, and it is now implementing the fourth strategic plan for the period of 2011-15.

Tanzania initiated its first five-year strategic plan in 1998/99 for the period 1998/99-2002/2003. It was prepared with the help of external consultants and focused basically on institutional and capacity building. The focus of the second strategic plan, prepared with both external and TRA efforts for the period of 2003/04-2007/08, aimed at making TRA investor and taxpayer friendly. The TRA's third strategic plan (2008/09-2012/13) was prepared on the basis of the bottom-up approach where field offices, all the stakeholders and development partners were involved actively in designing the plan. This plan strives to tackle the future challenges associated with the advancement of technology. Now

---

37   Strategic planning is adopted by organisations, other than tax administration, in different countries, including the United States, where the Government Performance and Results Act (GPRA) 1993 "requires Federal agencies to develop goals, objectives, related strategies and performance measures that gauge program results. GPRA also requires a description of the program evaluations used to establish or revise general goals and objectives." See Treasury Inspector General for Tax Administration, *Strategic Plan Fiscal Years 2009-2014*, p.7.

38   For selected strategic plans of SARAs, see OECD, *Tax Administration in OECD and Selected Non-OECD Countries: Comparative Information Series*, ch. 3, Paris, 2008, pp.58-75.

39   S.H. Wanyaka, "Report on Gender Budget Analysis of Taxation in Uganda, Focusing on Central Government Taxation Carried out by Uganda Revenue Authority," November 2003, p.22.

40   *Ibid.* p.23.

41   See www.ura.org.

TRA is in the process of formulating its fourth strategic plan for five years beginning in 2013/14.

Kenya adopted its first three-year strategic plan for 2000/01-2002/03. It implemented its second plan for 2003/04-2005/06, third plan for 2006/07-2008/09, fourth plan for 2009/10-2011/12 and it is now implementing its fifth strategic plan for the period 2012/13-2014/15. The RRA initiated its strategic plan in 2001 and is currently implementing its Medium Term Strategy for the period from 1 July 2010 to 30 June 2013. BPA has been implementing its first five-year plan for 2011-2015.

8.9 Summary

A modern, motivated, strong and efficient tax administration is required in order to implement the tax system in a proper and effective manner. In the absence of this, no matter how apparent tax policy appears to be, it becomes distorted and ineffective and fails to produce desired results. That is why there has been an increasing focus on the reform of tax administration in recent years all over the world, which comprises the reform of the organisational structure, the personnel system, the incentive package, tax procedures and automation.

EAC countries have made great progress over the past two decades in reforming their tax administration systems. They have taken tax administration outside the civil service and have established tax bodies as semi-autonomous organisations. EAC SARAs have been organised as unified tax administrations with a mixed organisational structure, where functional focus is combined with the taxpayer segment focus. SARAs are corporate bodies working as government agencies under the general supervision of the Finance Minister. They are responsible for assessing and collecting taxes, customs duties and a few specified non-tax sources. They also advise the Finance Ministers on tax policy and administration and revenue implications of new tax measures. These bodies have been implementing medium-term strategic plans that define their visions, missions, values, objectives, activities and performance indicators.move all non-tariff barriers relating to trade taking place within the Union. The establishment of the Customs Union is the first stage of the regional integration process in the EAC region.d income taxes of the EAC member states and there is a long way to go to fully harmonise the tax systems of these countries.

Chapter 9

Concluding Observations

9.1 Economic integration

EAC, established in 2000, is the fastest growing regional intergovernmental organisation of five East African Nations: Burundi, Kenya, Rwanda, Tanzania and Uganda. EAC member states are committed to integrate their economies with four pillars of integration, vis. customs union, common market, monetary union and political federation. While the customs union has been implemented, others are work in progress.

9.2 Customs union

In connection to the creation of the customs union, a Protocol for the Establishment of the Customs Union was signed in 2004 and the Customs Union was established in 2005. Under this arrangement, member states agreed to levy a 3-band common external tariff with a minimum rate of 0% on raw materials, a middle rate of 10% on semi-processed goods and a maximum rate of 25% on finished goods. They also agreed not to levy any internal tariff and to remove all non-tariff barriers relating to trade taking place within the Union. The establishment of the Customs Union is the first stage of the regional integration process in the EAC region.

9.3 Tax jurisdiction

EAC countries have adopted a unitary system of government where there are two tiers of government: national and local. Both the national and local governments are authorised to levy various taxes. All the EAC countries levy VAT, excise duties, customs duties, PIT and BPT at the national level while local governments are authorised to levy property based taxes, rental taxes, user charges and fees.

9.4 Value added tax

All EAC countries have adopted a standard destination based consumption type tax credit method VAT extended right through the retail level. EAC countries collect VAT at all stages in the process of production and distribution. This means that importers, manufacturers, wholesalers and retailers above the registration threshold are required to register for the purpose of VAT. They must collect tax on their sales and deduct the tax paid on their purchases from the tax collected on sales and remit the difference to the treasury as VAT. The rate structure of VAT in the EAC regions is simple. Rwanda, Tanzania and Uganda have adopted a single positive rate of 18% while Kenya has adopted a standard rate of 16% and a lower rate of 12% on the supply and import of electricity and fuels. While Burundi also levied VAT with a single rate of 18% until 2012, it has introduced a lower rate of 10% for agricultural products, live stocks and import of food. EAC countries zero-rate exports as well as some other specified commodities to relieve them from the burden of VAT. They have also exempted many goods and services from VAT.

9.5 Excise duties

EAC member countries levy excise duties on the domestic production, or import of excisable goods and provision of excisable services. Tobacco products, alcoholic beverages, vehicles, gasoline, and telecommunication are commonly specified as excisable items in the EAC countries. Burundi, Rwanda and Tanzania levy excise duties on an *ad valorem* basis on some items and on a specific basis on others. Similarly, Kenya levies *ad valorem* rates on some items, specific rates on others. Kenya also fixes rates on both specific and an *ad valorem* basis on some other items, whichever is the higher rate being the effective rate. EAC countries collect excise duties basically at the import/manufacturing point on excisable goods and supply of services in case of excisable services.

9.6 Customs duties

EAC countries do not levy internal tariff on the import of goods produced within EAC member states. They, however, do levy a three band common external tariff on imports from countries outside EAC region. The level of tariff depends upon the stage of finish of a product. For example, raw materials are subject to zero tariffs, semi-processed goods are subject to lower rate and finished goods are subject to higher tariff. EAC members have adopted the Harmonised System, which is required to be adopted by the member countries under the Protocol on the Establishment of the East African Customs Union. They follow the GATT valuation system for the determination of customs duties.

9.7 Personal income tax

EAC countries levy PIT on the taxable income that includes all sorts of income received for the provision of labour or capital or both, of whatever form or nature. Income sources are broadly divided into three categories as employment, business and investment/property income. EAC countries levy tax on the worldwide income of a resident taxpayer, but only on the income from domestic source in the case of a non-resident taxpayer. EAC countries have, in general, adopted a global system, where income received by a taxpayer is considered on a global basis, not on source by source basis, for tax purposes and subject to progressive tax rates. They, however, levy separate tax on some sources of income. They also levy presumptive tax and withholding taxes. Thus EAC PITs include features of both global and scheduler tax and can best be seen as a quasi-global system. PIT is levied on net income, which is obtained by deducting from the gross income business expenses and personal expenses. Besides, an initial amount of income is exempt from tax by means of a basic allowance/zero-rate bracket. PIT is levied with progressive rates in all EAC countries.

9.8 Business profit tax

BPT is levied on net income or profit of legal entities, which is calculated by deducting allowable business expenses from the gross income. All EAC countries, except Burundi, have adopted a general deduction system where they allow taxpayers to deduct all the business expenses incurred directly in earning the business income in the income year. Burundi, however, has adopted an itemised system of deduction, where the deductible items are specifically mentioned in the tax law and no deduction is allowed for any other item.

Cost of capital nature is not deductible since assets are used to generate income for more than one year. Instead, depreciation on capital assets may be deducted during the useful life of the assets. While EAC countries largely have adopted a pooled system of depreciation, Burundi has adopted an itemised system of depreciation where depreciable items are listed separately and depreciation rates are specified for each item in the tax law.

All the EAC countries allow taxpayers to carry over losses and offset them against profits in future years, but the carry-forward period varies from country to country. For example, while losses can be carried forward for 3 years in Burundi, they can be deducted from the profit in the next five years in Rwanda. Burundi also allows carry-back losses for 4 years.

Resident companies are required to pay tax on both domestic as well as foreign sources, while for non-resident companies only income from domestic source is taken into account in all EAC countries except Burundi where tax is levied only on domestic source income in case of all companies, resident or non-resident. EAC countries generally levy BPT at a flat rate.

9.9 Intergovernmental fiscal relations

EAC countries have adopted a unitary system of government where there are two tiers of government, national and local. There are similarities as well as differences in the taxes levied at the local level in the EAC countries. Local governments levy property taxes which are in line with the principles of local taxation and international best practices. In Rwanda and Uganda local governments levy rent taxes. Local governments also levy user charges and some fees. There are also some country specific taxes levied by the local government of EAC countries.

Various levels of government have the authority to generate their own sources of revenue and decide how to use their revenue to provide public services. As these countries are implementing decentralisation programs, they have been transferring more and more expenditure responsibilities to the sub national governments. As the local governments know the requirements of their constituents better than the national governments, they can tailor programs to match the demand of their constituency. This is expected to enhance efficiency. However, tax assignments in these countries seem inappropriate since major revenue sources are limited to the national level but they have not been developed as shared taxes. As a result, there is a huge gap between demand and supply of fiscal resources at the sub national level, which are met mainly by inter-governmental transfers that cover almost 90% of all local government spending, while local governments' own source revenues and local government borrowings account for a nominal share of local financial resources.

9.10 Tax administration

EAC member states have established semi-autonomous revenue authorities to implement their tax systems. They are organised as unified tax administrations with a mixed organisational structure, where functional focus is combined with the taxpayer segment focus. EAC tax administrations have been implementing medium-term corporate plans that define their visions, missions, values, objectives, activities and performance indicators.

9.11 Summing-up

EAC member states have been trying to harmonise their tax systems. Their national tax systems are pretty much rationalised as these countries levy limited broad based taxes and there are no nuisance taxes, which is the main thrust of the modern tax reform. As stated above, while customs duties are fully harmonised, VATs are also largely synchronised. There are, however, striking differences in the structure and operation of excise duties and income taxes of the EAC member states and there is a long way to go to fully harmonise the tax systems of these countries.

Index

Select Bibliography

AM Center for Public Policy Studies and International Tax Investment Center (2007), Special Report on Addressing Harmonization of Excise Regimes in the East African Community: Petroleum, Alcohol, Tobacco, Soft Drinks and Mobile Communication, www.iticnet.org.

African Development Bank Group (2010), Domestic Resource Mobilization for Poverty Reduction in East Africa: Rwanda Case Study, Regional Department East A (OREA), November.

African Development Bank Group (2010), Domestic Resource Mobilization for Poverty Reduction in East Africa: Burundi Case Study, Regional Development East A (OREA), November.

Alarie, Benjamin and Richard M. Bird (2011), "Canada", in G. Bizioli and C. Sacchetto (edits.), Tax Aspects of Fiscal Federalism: A Comparative Analysis, International Bureau of Fiscal Documentation, Amsterdam.

Bahl, Roy (2011). Taxing Soft Drinks, International Studies Program Working Paper 11-06, Andrew Young School of Policy Studies, Georgia State University, Atlanta.

Bahl, Roy (2000), Intergovernmental Transfers in Developing and Transition Countries: Principles and Practice, Municipal Finance, Background Series 2, The World Bank, Washington DC.

Balassone, Fabrizio, Daniele Franco, and Stefania Zotteri (2002), "Fiscal Rules for Sub-national Governments, What Lessons from EMU Countries?," A Paper prepared for the Conference on "Rules-Based Macroeconomic Policies in Emerging Market Economies" jointly organized by the IMF and the World Bank, Oaxaca Mexico, February 14-16.

Bird, Richard M. (2003), "Local and Regional Revenues: Realities and Prospects," in Richard M. Bird and Francois Vaillancourt (edits.), The World Bank, Washington DC, 2006.

Bird, Richard M. (1993), "Threading the Fiscal Labyrinth: Some Issues in Fiscal Decentralization", National Tax Journal, Vol. 46, No. 2, pp.207-227.

Boadway, Robin and Anwar Shah (2009), Fiscal Federalism, Principles and Practices of Multiorder Governance, Cambridge University Press, Cambridge.

Boschmann, Nina (2009), Development Partners Working Group on Local Governance and Decentralization DPWG-LGD, Fiscal Decentralization and Options for Donor Harmonization, Berlin.

British-American Tobacco (2011), "Excise on Tobacco Products" Regional Public Private Dialogue on Harmonization of Domestic Taxes in the EAC. East African Business Council and the EAC Secretariat in collaboration with the TradeMark East Africa, Africa Capacity Building Foundation and the International Financial Corporation as part of the Network of Reformers in Dar es Salaam, from 11th -12th November.

Burundi, Government of (2009). Burundi Revenue Authority Law.

CIA. The World Fact Book. East Africa Facts and Figures, https://www.cia.gov/library/publications/the-world-factbook.

Cnossen, Sijbren (2006), "Alcohol Taxation and Regulation in the European Union," CESIFO Working Paper No. 1821, Category 1: Public Finance, Presented at CESIFO Conference in Public Sector Economics.

Cnossen, Sijbren (2010). Excise Taxation in Australia. Chapter 10 in Australia's Future Tax and Transfer Policy Conference, Melbourne Institute.

Cnossen, Sijbren (2001). "How Should Tobacco Be Taxed In EU-Accession Countries?" CESIFO Working Paper No. 539.

Crandall, B. & M. Kidd (2009), A Toolkit For Implementing A Revenue Authority (RA), Caribbean Regional Technical Assistance Center, International Monetary Fund.

Commonwealth Association of Tax Administrators (2006), "Implementing Large Taxpayer Units," available at www.catatax.org/upiloads/051006/LTU.report.20.4.06.pdf.

Commonwealth Local Government Forum (CLFG). Country Profile: Uganda, the Local Government System in Uganda, available at www.clfg.org.uk.

Diamond, John, George Zodrow and Robert Carroll (March 2013), Macroeconomic Effects of Lower Corporate Income Tax Rates Recently Enacted Abroad, Ernst and Young LLP.

Due, John F. (1963), Government Finance: An Economic Analysis, Richard D. Irwin, Inc., Homewood, Illinois.

EAC (2003). The East African Excise Management Act, Section 36.

EAC (2012), "East African Community Facts and Figures," EAC Secretariat, Arusha, Tanzania available at www.eac.int.

EAC (2013), "East African Community Facts and Figures," EAC, Arusha, Tanzania available at www.eac.int.

EAC (East African Community) (2012), Customs Post Clearance Audit Manual, EAC Secretariat, Arusha, January.

EAC, "History of EAC," http://www.eac.int/index.

EAC, "What is the common market?" http://www.eac.int/commonmarket/what-it-is.html.

EAC (2012), "Tanzania becomes first partner state to ratify EAC monetary union protocol," http://www.eac.int/index.php?option=com_content&view=article&id=1601:-tanzania-becomes-first-partner-state-to-ratify-eac-monetary-union-protocol&catid=146:press-releases&Itemid=194. East African Community Secretariat, Arusha, Tanzania, September.

East African, The. "East Africa dithers over the Double Taxation Agreement, loses investment" 11 August 2014, http://www.theeastafrican.co.ke/news/-/2558/2415362/-/5m0tn6z/-/index.html.

Eissa, Nada O. & William Jack (2009), Tax Reform in Kenya: Policy and Administrative Issues. Initiative for Policy Dialogue Working Paper Series, Georgetown University, October.

EU (2008). EU Council Directive 2008/118/EC of 16 December.

EU (1992). EU Council Directive 92/12/EEC of 25 February 1992 on the general arrangements for products subject to excise duty and on the holding, movement and monitoring of such products.

Fjeldstand, O.H. (2002), Fighting Fiscal Corruption: The Case of the Tanzania Revenue Authority, Chr. Michelson Institute Development Studies and Human Rights, Working Paper 2002:3.

Fjeldstand, O.-H. (2001), Intergovernmental Fiscal Relations in Developing Countries: A Review of Issues, WP 2001:11, Chr. Michelsen Institute Development Studies and Human Rights.

Gallagher, M. (2005), Benchmarking Tax System, Public Administration and Development, See http://frp2.org/english/Portals/0/Library/Tax%20Administration/Benchmarking%20Tax%20Systems%20-%20Full%20Text.pdf.

Gill, J.B.S. (2003), "The Nuts and Bolts of Revenue Administration Reform," Lead Public Sector Management Specialist Europe and Central Asia Region, 2003, available athttp://siteresources.worldbank.org/INTTPA/Resources/NutsBolts.pdf.

Gillis, Malcolm (edit.) (1971), Fiscal Reforms for Columbia (Richard A. Musgrave Commission Report), The Law School of Harvard University, Cambridge.

Glenday, Graham (1991) "On Safari in Kenya: from Sales Tax to Value Added Tax" International VAT Monitor, December.

Gunlicks, Arthur (2005), "German Federalism: Theory and Developments, German Federalism and Recent Reform Efforts", German Law Journal, 06 No. 10, pp.1283-1296.

Hewitt, Daniel P. (1991), "Transfers to Local Government," in Ke-young Chu and Richard Hemming (edits.) Public Expenditure Handbook, A Guide to Public Expenditure Policy Issues in Developing Countries, Government Expenditure Analysis Division, Fiscal Affairs Department, International Monetary Fund, Washington DC.

Hutton, Eric, Mick Thackray, & Philippe Wingender (2014) Revenue Administration Gap Analysis Program – The Value-Added Tax Gap, April, available at:

IMF (2013). IMF Country Report.13/25, January.

IMF (2013). IMF Country Report. 13/12, January.

IMF (2012). IMF Country Report. 12/300, November.

IMF (2006). IMF Country Report. 06/311.

IMF (1998). IMF Country Report. 98/61, June.

International VAT Monitor (2000).

International VAT Monitor (December 1999), 10, 6.

International VAT Monitor (June 1999).

International VAT Monitor (September/October 1996).

International VAT Monitor (1995), 6, 2.

International VAT Monitor (October 1990).

International VAT Monitor (September 1990).

International VAT Monitor (January 1990).

Jenkins, Glenn & Rup Khadka (2000), "Modernization of Tax Administration in Low-Income Countries: The Case of Nepal," CAER II Discussion Paper 68, Harvard Institute for International Development (HIID), Cambridge.

Jenkins, Glenn P. (1994), "International: Modernization of Tax Administrations: Revenue Boards and Privatization as Instruments for Changes", Bulletin, February 1994, pp.75-80, available at www.queensjdiexec.org/publications/qed_dp_113.pdf.

Kay, J.A. & King, M.A. (1990), The British Tax System, Oxford University Press, Oxford.

Kee, James Edwin (2003), Fiscal Decentralization: Theory as Reform, VIII Congreso International del CLAD sobre la Reforma del Estado Y de la Administración Publica, Panama, 28-31 October.

Kelly, Roy (1998), "Intergovernmental Revenue Allocation Theory and Practice: Application to Nepal," Development Discussion Paper No. 624, Harvard Institute for International Development, Harvard University, Cambridge.

Kenya, Government of (1995). Kenya Revenue Authority Act.

Kenya, Government of (1989). Schedules II (exempt goods) and III (exempt services). VAT Act 1989.

Kenya, Government of (1974). Section 77. Income Tax Act 1974.

Khadka, Rup Bahadur (2014), "VAT in the East African Community", International VAT Monitor, March/April, pp.89-92.

Khadka, Rup Bahadur (2014), "Tax Administration in the East African Community", Bulletin for International Taxation, Vol. 68, No.4/5, published online on March 26, 2014.

Lent, George E. (1977), "Corporation Income Tax Structure in Developing Countries", IMF Staff Papers, 25(3).

Mann, Arthur J. (2004), "Are Semi-Autonomous Revenue Authorities The Answer To Tax Administration Problems In Developing Countries?" – A Practical Guide, Fiscal Reform in Support of Trade Liberalization Project, available at http://pdf.usaid.gov/pdf_docs/Pnadc978.pdf.

Martinez-Vazquez, Jorge, Andrey Timofeev & Jameson Boex (2006), Reforming Regional-Local Finance in Russia, The World Bank, Washington, DC.

McLure, Charles E. & Jorge Martinez-Vazquez, The Assignment of Revenues and Expenditures in Intergovernmental Fiscal Relations, World Bank Institute's Decentralization Homepage (www.worldbank.org/decentralization).

McLure, Charles E., Jr., & Santiago Pardo R. (1992), "Improving the Administration of the Colombian Income Tax, 1986-88", Richard M. Bird and Milka Casanegra de Jantscher, (edits.), Improving Tax Administration in Developing Countries, International Monetary Fund, Washington DC.

Mtange, Patrick (2012). ICPAK Position Paper on the VAT Bill 2012, Institute of Certified Public Accountants of Kenya, Nairobi.

Musgrave, Richard A. (1959), The Theory of Public Finance, A Study in Public Economy, McGraw-Hill Book Company, New York, Toronto and London, Inc.

Oates, Wallace E. (1999), "An Essay on Fiscal Federalism", Journal of Economic Literature, Vol. XXXVII.

OECD (2008), Tax Administration in OECD and Selected Non-OECD Countries: Comparative Information Series, ch. 3, Paris.

OECD Tax Policy Studies (2006), Fundamental Reform of Personal Income Tax No.13, Organization for Economic Cooperation and Development, Paris.

OECD (2011), "Special Features: Trends in Personal Income Tax and Employee Social Security Contribution Schedules", Taxing Wages 2011, Organization for Economic Cooperation and Development, Paris, p.44. See http://www.oecd.org/tax/tax-policy/50131824.pdf.

OECD (2005), Note 4, "Tax/Benefit Policies and Parental Work and Care Decision" in Babies and Bosses: Reconciling Work and Family Life, Vol.4, Organization for Economic Cooperation Development, Paris, 2005, p.12.

OECD Tax Policy Studies, Fundamental Reform of Personal Income Tax No.13, Organization for Economic Cooperation and Development, Paris, 2006, p. 62.

Preece, Rob (2008). Key Controls in the Administration of Excise Duties. World Customs Journal, 2, 1.

PWC (2013). Doing Business: Know Your Taxes, East African Tax Guide 2012/13.

Rao, M. Govinda & Tapas K. Sen (2011), "Federalism and Fiscal Reform in India," Working Paper No. 2011-84, National Institute of Public Finance and Policy, New Delhi.

Sri Lanka, Government of (1991). Report of the Taxation Commission 1990, Government Publication Bureau, Colombo.

Rosenow, Sheri & Brain J. O'Shea (2010), A Handbook on WTO Customs Valuation Agreement, World Trade Organization.

Rwanda, Government of. Law No. 08/2009 of 27 April 2009 on Determining the Organization, Functioning and Responsibilities of the Rwanda Revenue Authority.

Rwanda, Government of (2006). Excise Law No. 26/2006 of 27/05/2006 Determining and Establishing Consumption Tax on Some Imported and Locally Manufactured Products in Rwanda.

Rwanda, Government of (2005). Section 6. Laws on Direct Taxes on Income 2005.

Rwanda, Government of (2005). Article 20 of Law No. 16/2005 of 18/08/2005 on Direct Taxes on Income.

Rwanda, Government of (2010). Article 86. VAT Act.

Shah, Anwar (1994), The Reform of Intergovernmental Fiscal Relations in Developing and Emerging Market Economies, The World Bank, Washington DC.

Shome, Parthasarathi (2012), Tax Shastra, Administrative Reforms in India, United Kingdom and Brazil, BS Books, New Delhi.

Simbyakula, Robert Ngosa (1990), "Zambia: Tax Treatment of the Family" (1990), Bulletin for International Fiscal Documentation, Vol. 44, October.

Smith, Adam (1776), The Wealth of Nations, Rpt. Introduction by Robert Reicb, The Modern Library, New York, 2000.

Smith, Stephen (2003). Taxes on Road Transport in Southern African Countries, Revised version of a paper presented at the South African Conference on Excise Taxation, Pretoria, South Africa, 11-13 June, p.1.

Stewart, Miranda (2011), Chapter 4 Australia, in Benjamin Alarie and Richard M. Bird, "Canada", in G. Bizioli and C. Sacchetto (edits), Tax Aspects of Fiscal Federalism, A Comparative Analysis, International Bureau of Fiscal Documentation, Amsterdam.

Sunley, Emil M., Ayda Yurekli & Frank J. Chaloupka (2000), The Design, Administration, and Potential Revenue of Tobacco Excises, Chapter 17, in Prabhat Jha & Frank Chaloupka (editors), Tobacco Control in Developing Countries, Oxford University Press, Oxford.

Taliercio, R. Jr. (2004), "Designing Performance: The Semi-Autonomous Revenue Authority Model in Africa and Latin America," World Bank Policy Research Working Paper 3423.

Tanzania, Government of (2010). Budget Speech 2009/10.

Tanzania, Government of (2005). Budget Speech 2004/05.

Tanzania, Government of (2004). Section 77. Income Tax Act 2004.

Tanzania, Government of (2004). Section 70. Income Tax Act 2004.

Tanzania, The United Republic of, President's Office (2003), Final Report: Developing a System of Inter-governmental Grants in Tanzania, A report prepared for Local Government Reform Program by Georgia State University Andrew Young School of Public Policy, Atlanta.

Tanzania, Government of (1997). Schedule II (Special Relief in Schedule III). VAT Act 1997.

Tanzania, Government of (1995). Tanzania Revenue Authority Act 1995. http://www.tra.go.tz/index.php/withholding-tax.

Tax News Service (2007, March 7).

Terra, Ben J. M. (1996), "Chapter 8 Excises", Victor Thuronyi, (edit.), Tax Law Design and Drafting, Vol. 1, International Monetary Fund, Washington, DC.

TradeMark East Africa. http://www.trademarkea.com/news/double-taxation-stumbling-block-towards-trade-boost-eac/

Tiebout, Charles M. (1956), "A Pure Theory of Local Expenditures", The Journal of Political Economy, Vol. 64, No.5.

Uganda, Government of (1999), Local Government Finance Commission, Introduction of Equalization Grant, Analysis and Recommendations, Kampala.

Uganda, Government of (1997). Section 81. Income Tax Act 1997.

Uganda, Government of (1996). Schedule II. VAT Act 1996.

Uganda, Government of. (1991). Uganda Revenue Authority Act 1991.

UNCTAD Trust Fund for Trade Facilitation Negotiations Technical Note No. 21, Automated System for Customs Data ASYCUDA.

UNCTAD Trust Fund on Trade Facilitation Negotiations, Technical Note No. 12, Risk Management for Customs Control, Produced jointly by the World Customs Organization and UNCTAD.

UNCTAD Trust Fund on Trade Facilitation Negotiations, Technical Note No. 5, Post-Clearance Audit, Produced jointly by the World Customs Organization and UNCTAD.

UNCTAD Trust Fund for Trade Facilitation Negotiations Technical Note No. 3, Use of Customs Automation Systems.

United States Agency for International Development (2011), Customs Modernization Handbook, Post-Clearance Audit Program, A Businesslike Approach To Customs Control, Produced by Nathan Associates Inc. for the United States Agency for International Development. http://egateg.usaid.gov/collecting-taxes.

Wanyaka, S.H. (2003), "Report on Gender Budget Analysis of Taxation in Uganda, Focusing on Central Government Taxation Carried out by Uganda Revenue Authority."

Zake, Justin (2011), "Customs Administration Reform and Modernization in Anglophone Africa – Early 1990s to Mid-2010," IMF Working Paper WP/11/184, International Monetary Fund, Washington DC.

Zake, Justin O.S. (1990), "The Introduction of VAT in Uganda: Avoiding the Great Ghanaian Debacle", International VAT Monitor, 7, 2.

Zimmermann, Horst (2011), Roles versus functions for the federal middle level: A structure and a growth perspective, Working Paper Series No.1, Faculty of Economics, Toyo University, Tokyo.

Printed in the United States
By Bookmasters